OKLAHOMA HERITAGE QUILTS

A SAMPLING OF QUILTS MADE IN OR BROUGHT TO OKLAHOMA BEFORE 1940

OKLAHOMA HERITAGE QUILTS

A Sampling of Quilts Made in or Brought to Oklahoma before 1940

OKLAHOMA QUILT HERITAGE PROJECT

Photography by:
Gene and Patricia Higgins, Norman, Oklahoma

Editors:
Jane Amstutz Harnden, Edmond, Oklahoma
Pamela Frazee Woolbright, Oklahoma City, Oklahoma

"Dedicated to quilters known and unknown"

PREFACE

Quilts provide a unique vantage point from which one can view history, traditions and social patterns. The Oklahoma Quilt Heritage survey and this resulting book are a reflection of the people who settled Oklahoma and were part of her formative years up to 1940. Oklahomans' lives, customs and values are revealed and their stories told through artifacts they made and left as legacies–their quilts.

The Oklahoma Quilt Heritage Project was conceived in 1984 and carried out by members of a non-profit guild of quilt lovers who cherish these vintage textiles. During the past decade a number of states have conducted quilt documentation/registration projects. In Oklahoma this has been done by a group of volunteers who felt the project was too important and the timing too critical to wait until funding from government or business entities was available. At the outset it was determined that the service should be free to all citizens and offered in numerous locales.

Due to economic necessity, many quilts made in Oklahoma's early years were created from feedsacks and portions of worn clothing, and it was feared that these artifacts might not be saved or cherished by another generation unless a deliberate effort was made to affirm their value. Therefore, working on a shoestring budget–which thrifty quilters of the past would have applauded–the project team members utilized available resources and skills to accomplish the statewide registration.

After almost three years of study, textile research, fund raising, planning and preparation, the Oklahoma QUILT DAYS started in August, 1987. During the next sixteen months, the team of ten traveled over 26,000 miles to register quilts in nineteen registration sites and was assisted by 502 community volunteers representing quilters, quiltlovers and persons interested in history. The cities and towns for these registration days were carefully selected to be within a reasonable driving distance for all persons across the state.

Owners of vintage quilts responded and over 4,000 quilts "made in or brought to Oklahoma before 1940" went through the process of being measured, photographed and examined so that notes could be made about the design, fabric and techniques used by the maker. The person bringing the quilt provided information about the quiltmaker: dates of birth and death, places of residence, when, where and why the quilt was made, and how it came to the present owner. Information was recorded about when the quilt came to Oklahoma, who brought it and why they came. Interesting insights about the state's early settlers can be seen in this data. While the quilts registered constitute only a small percentage of the vintage quilts in existence within Oklahoma, they are an excellent representative sampling. The records and data (quiltmaker histories and color slides) obtained through this project will be placed in the archives of the Oklahoma Historical Society to augment this aspect of the state's history.

Oklahoma Quilt Heritage team members feel honored and privileged to have been invited into people's remembrances of their private lives, and thus allowed to glimpse events and relationships that shaped the person. The quilts selected for this book were not chosen because they were the "prettiest, oldest, or most important ones registered"; rather, we felt they were representative of the total in terms of pattern design and fabric, locale and family story. They reveal family records, customs, lifestyles, economic conditions, and values of the various ethnic and racial groups in territorial and early statehood years. Hopefully, all families with Oklahoma lineage will find their own heritage affirmed as they read the following pages.

A QUILT DAY volunteer, Betty Gilliam of Stillwater, captured the essence of the project when she wrote the following reflections one month after a registration day.

The Stillwater Quilt Heritage Day was a delight to the eye and to the mind. I worked with other volunteers helping participants fill out information sheets about their quilts. After a month of thought, I realize that while I greatly enjoyed the visual delights of that day, the more significant, lasting effect is in the personal memories and thoughts the day evoked.

My grandmother, of Cherokee descent, was a wonderful quilter. I have memories of pins on the floor and pieces of quilt frame leaning against the wall. She taught me to sew doll clothes on her treadle Singer. I loved her very much, but in my teenage impudence I was critical of her limited formal education and her lack of worldly knowledge.

Grandmother died as I was becoming an adult—before I learned to appreciate all she had to offer. I have only one quilt of hers made as a wedding present to me. It is "too young" to have been part of QUILT DAY, but Grandmother became part of that day. As I listened to the quilt owners tell their stories, some with pictures of the quiltmakers, I became very proud of Oklahoma's heritage and my family's part in it.

Our busy world today leads to fragmented families, to moving away from tradition, to embracing newness and change. In contrast, this day gave me a sense of continuity and a good feeling about my family's place in history. I have greater respect for those men and women who helped our state grow. I have a more complete image of my grandmother—she led a busy, really rather ordinary life, but left wonderful gifts to me and her other grandchildren: her sense of ethics and hard work, her love of family, our Cherokee heritage, and her beautiful sewing skills.

If readers of this book derive a sense of identity with their own past and feel their family's story is affirmed, and if they gain an appreciation for the artistry and love that is expressed by quiltmakers through their stitches, this book will have achieved our goal.

Jane Amstutz Harnden, Coordinator
Oklahoma QUILT DAYS Project

ACKNOWLEDGEMENTS

No project of this magnitude is completed without the assistance of many people. As the Oklahoma Quilt Heritage registration process concludes, we wish to express our gratitude to:

Central Oklahoma Quilters Guild, Inc. which authorized initiation of the project and who, with the Oklahoma State Quilters Guild, Inc. provided major funding;

quilt guilds and groups in Oklahoma that assisted with finances, time, and energy;

staff of National Cowboy Hall of Fame and Western Heritage Center and Oklahoma Historical Society for assistance in research;

community organizations, churches and business firms that provided facilities, equipment and funding for local QUILT DAYS;

the 502 volunteers across the state who performed the physical labor of assisting in the nineteen QUILT DAYS;

the thousands of people who made the effort to bring their quilts to be registered and thus entrusted us with their treasured artifacts and the stories of their lives;

last, but by no means least, our families. We wish to recognize and thank our spouses and children who have supported this project financially, and who have freed us of home responsibilities so that we could travel and spend the countless hours this volunteer effort required.

This project has affirmed our conviction that money cannot buy the most valuable things in life. There has been no financial payment for those involved in this undertaking but we have been richly rewarded by the feeling that comes when something worthwhile is accomplished, by visiting parts of the state that were new to us, by seeing beautiful quilts and by hearing the marvelous stories of family and community relationships, and most of all, by meeting wonderful people in every QUILT DAY site!

The Oklahoma Quilt Heritage Team

Jane Amstutz Harnden, Edmond
Pamela Frazee Woolbright, Oklahoma City
Trudy Mitchell Gullo, Oklahoma City
Betty Jo Schroder Haines, Hydro
Thelma Hill Baker, Stillwater
Patricia Duerksen Higgins, Norman
Susanne Sanford Rose, Stillwater
Lorraine Moore Lear, Del City
Billie Seward Hodgell, Norman
Jeri-Alynn Rhoads McGee, Oklahoma City

CONTENTS

INTRODUCTION

Each of the quilts in this book is a unique artifact which when considered as a total tells a much larger story. Quilts reflect the lives of people and collectively allow us to view the society they represent. To be fully appreciated and understood, quilts need to be viewed within the framework of locale and time for each is a product of its own distinctive era, thus influenced by the tides of civilization. The quilts in this book tell the story of the early people of Oklahoma.

Not only are the quilts in this book visually representative but the stories they tell are for the most part typical. The narratives are of family units and orphans; of homes that were tents, sod houses and ornate mansions; of farmers, ranchers and businessmen; of new immigrants, freed slaves and Native Americans; in short, a cross-section of Americans. Perhaps the most unique factor in the Oklahoma story is the relatively short span of time into which the settlement process was telescoped. The time of the first permanent settlement of Indian tribes until statehood in 1907 was less than seventy-five years.

While this book is about the state's legacy of quilts, it is impossible to tell that account without sharing a bit of Oklahoma's topography and history. Oklahoma contains every type of land from desert to swamp, from mountain plateaus to windswept plains. For our purposes, we will generalize to state that the land can be roughly divided by a line north to south lying midway across the state, which was referred to in early writings as the "cross timbers." To the east of this line the terrain is wooded, hilly, and there are many natural streams; to the west, the land is more prairie-like.

Permanent settlement came first to the eastern half of the Indian Territory in about 1830 when the United States government forcibly moved land-owning, agrarian Cherokee, Choctaw, Creek and Chickasaw tribes from the southeastern states to this land west of the Mississippi River. The move was tragic and referred to in some of the individual quiltmakers' stories as the "Trail of Tears" or "Choctaw Removal." With permission from the tribal leaders, white families could settle in the various Indian Nations and did so in the role of traders, teachers, ministers and farmers. Black families came during this period also, for many of the southern Indians had owned plantations and slaves. They were not allowed to own slaves in the new territory but many former slaves were named as tribal members and came in the exodus.

The western half of the area remained for the most part unoccupied, but was subsequently taken away from the tribes mentioned above and declared available for settling more tribes. This time the Indians were brought from a nonagrarian, nomadic, hunting lifestyle on the western plains and told they were to become land owners and farmers. Sections were assigned to various tribal groups and the people were forcibly brought by government troops to their new homes.

This phase lasted only a few years. Then other people wanted to obtain the land for ranching, business expansion, or farming; and Congress was pressured to open this last frontier area for homesteading. Laws were passed that allotted specific acreage to individual Indians rather than to tribal holdings as in the past, and the rest of the land was declared 'unowned' and available for settlement. Thus began a series of unprecedented land openings.

The land was surveyed, divided into sections of 640 acres and then into townships containing thirty-six sections. Land was set aside in each township for schools. In areas designated to become towns, property was laid out in city lots. Advertisement was made nationwide that on a specified date at

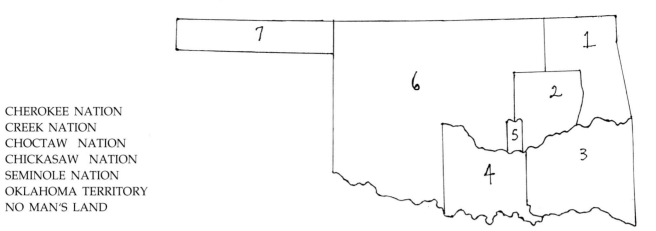

1 CHEROKEE NATION
2 CREEK NATION
3 CHOCTAW NATION
4 CHICKASAW NATION
5 SEMINOLE NATION
6 OKLAHOMA TERRITORY
7 NO MAN'S LAND

a given hour persons would be allowed to enter the area and claim 160 acres of land or a city lot with the stipulation that they file their claim and build a place of abode, thus making it their home. The first Run was scheduled for April 22, 1889, in Unassigned Lands in Central Oklahoma. It is estimated that 50,000 people participated that day, lining up along the boundary in every conceivable mode of conveyance or on foot. At noon when the cannon sounded, everyone went as fast as possible to claim a piece of land. By evening towns had sprung up where in the morning there had only been a train station and few meagre tents or buildings. It was "instant settlement" of an area--unique in the nation. Between 1889 and 1906, a total of thirteen areas in Oklahoma Territory were opened for settlement by runs or by more conventional methods of lotteries, sealed bids or allottments.

All who came to this new territory had a common need–to establish a home. For those whose land had no trees, their only alternative was to dig into a hillside to create a "dugout" or to cut chunks of the prairie and stack them brick-fashion with the roots holding the soil in place, making a "sod house." Many of the stories of this book refer to living in a sod house or dugout with a dirt floor. This was not a sign of poverty in pioneer days but simply the prairie equivalent of the log cabin housing used in other parts of the country by early settlers. Most sod houses and dugouts were replaced after one or two years with a small frame house, usually consisting of two to four rooms. If the family prospered and times were good, the next residence might well be a multi-story, large Victorian style frame house.

Wrestling a living in a new territory was a challenge in its own right whether one was a businessman living in town or a farmer on the land. In addition to the very unique and dramatic settlement pattern, other factors affected these two distinct territories which united to become the nation's forty-sixth state in 1907.

The Indians of Indian Territory raised wheat and other grains in small plots for family use but it was the new settlers in Oklahoma Territory who made the land conform to their needs. With the arrival of the German-Russian immigrants with their hard winter wheat, farming became a big business. Cotton was an important crop in early Oklahoma and was raised both as a cash crop and for home use.

The discovery of vast reserves of oil and gas under the land brought instant riches and its resulting problems to some areas. The stock market crash of 1929 affected life in Oklahoma as it did lives across the nation, but the depression years were extended in the midwest by a severe, five year drought that changed the top soil to blowing dust, creating the devastating "dust bowl years."

Education was a high priority with almost all the diverse groups who arrived. Schools with well trained teachers were established in Indian Territory and provisions were made for higher education. One room country schools offering an eighth grade education were the norm for the settlers in Oklahoma Territory. Taught by persons whose own education was little more than their students, pupils obtained an amazingly good education, perhaps because their desire and determination were so great.

World War II changed the economy, employment opportunities, lifestyles and educational opportunities. Oklahoma witnessed a shift from agrarian to urban population base, giving impetus to water control and the creation of dams and lakes, but this is another story.

The quilts in this book and the stories they tell reflect only the foundation years of the state--prior to 1940.

"Waiting for the Run." Oklahoma Historical Society photo

Chapter I

FAMILY TRADITIONS

When moving to a new locale, people take with them treasured mementos to give a sense of continuity and help them remember family and friends. The families who settled this new territory had a wide variety of ethnic backgrounds and felt the need to keep their traditions alive so the heritage could be passed to the next generation. In addition to the utility quilts required for daily use, people brought special quilts to symbolize their ties with the past.

The Road To Oklahoma

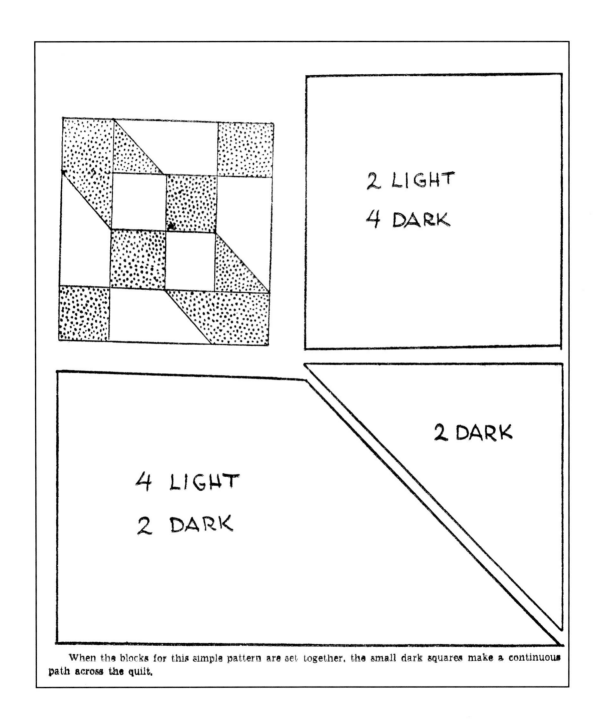

2 LIGHT
4 DARK

2 DARK

4 LIGHT
2 DARK

When the blocks for this simple pattern are set together, the small dark squares make a continuous path across the quilt.

IRISH CHAIN

Maker: **Tabatha Morton Gholson. Made in Kentucky, circa 1820.**

Inscribed: **Initials "T.M." cross-stitched on back.**

Owner: **Marilyn Brown, great-great-great-great-granddaughter.**

Pieced: **99" x 86"; cotton: navy and gold prints on white solid; hand quilted.**

Attached to the back of this quilt was the following: "This quilt was pieced by Tabitha Morton Gholson for her son John Morton Gholson. Left to his daughter Tabitha Gholson McFarland in 1865 then to her daughter Mollie McFarland Brown then to her son Arthur McFarland Brown."

Family records show that this Irish Chain quilt was brought by Mollie McFarland Brown to Tulsa, Indian Territory, in 1905. The quilt passed from her son Arthur to grandson Arthur Harrison Brown who left it to his daughter, the present owner.

WREATH OF ROSES ➤

Maker: **Sarah Elizabeth Shultz Miller (1826-death date unknown). Made at Washington, Rappahannock County, Virginia, 1839.**

Owner: **Ruth Montgomery.**

Appliqued and pieced: **92" x 76"; cotton: red, green and yellow; hand quilted.**

At age thirteen, Sarah Elizabeth Shultz had mastered the art of applique and fine quilting as evidenced by this masterpiece with its white background area filled with triple rows of tiny stitches, ten per inch. Warmth was not a critical need in the southern states, and from earliest times their quilts featured graceful, pictorial applique. Workmanship was stressed, as these artifacts were destined to be featured as coverlets rather than utility bedding. Quilts like this one were frequently included in the trousseau of southern belles when they married.

In 1920, Parrish Elizabeth Etter, granddaughter of the maker, brought the elegant quilt to Bartlesville, Oklahoma. Parrish Etter was the wife of Dr. Forrest Etter, an early day Washington County physician. Their stately country home called "The Evergreens" was surrounded by a grove of large evergreens and was appointed throughout with ornate, family heirloom furnishings.

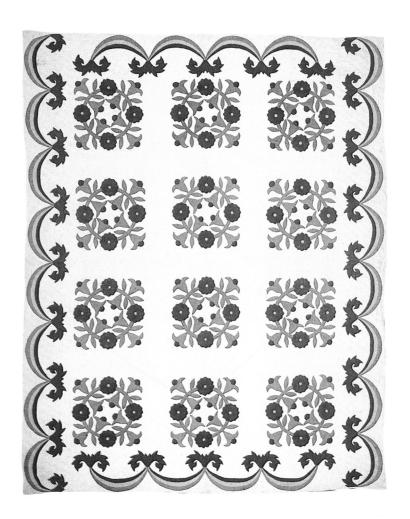

MOUNTAIN LILY

Maker: **Susanna Gall Shank (1827-1925). Made in Philippi, West Virginia, circa 1849.**

Owner: **Teresa Ann Littau, descendant.**

Pieced and appliqued: **91" x 70"; cotton: red, yellow, green and white; hand quilted.**

As a young bride, Susan Shank made this quilt for herself and her husband Jacob who had served with Robert E. Lee during the Mexican War in 1846. The men remained friends and the Shanks planned to name their fifth child born in 1861 in his honor. The baby was a girl and they named her Rosa Lee.

When Rosa married Austin B. Ward in 1879, they went west by covered wagon and settled in Lajunta, Colorado, living first in a dugout, then a black adobe house. Rosa Shank Ward and her husband made a final move to Cleo Springs, Oklahoma, in 1926. The quilt made by Rosa's mother went with the family each time and has now been passed through six generations.

CROWN OF THORNS VARIATION ➤

Maker: **Unknown. Made in Tennessee or Kentucky, circa 1850.**

Owners: **Lulu Mae and Ellis Cowan.**

Pieced: **82" x 71"; cotton: blue print and white solid; hand quilted in blue and white thread.**

After service in the Confederate Army, an unknown ancestor of the quilt owners returned to his home near Knoxville, Tennessee, bringing this quilt and another with him. It is not known how these came into his possession.

The quilt was brought to Oklahoma in 1915 by E.E. Cowan, a teacher and administrator, and has been passed down through four generations of the family.

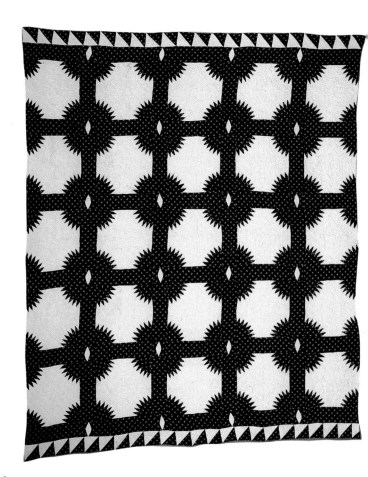

STAR OF BETHELEHEM

Maker: **Sidney Sophia Cather Gore (1828-1906). Made in Gore, Virginia, 1849.**

Inscribed: "Sidney Sophia Gore 1849" in cross stitch embroidery.

Owner: **Martha Burns Boren (Mrs. Horace C. Boren).**

Pieced and reverse applique: 91" x 91"; cotton; blue, red, yellow and green on white; hand quilted.

Sidney Cather Gore created her Mosaic and Star of Bethlehem quilts at "Valley Home," Gore, Virginia, about a decade before the South was engulfed by the tides of the Civil War. Located just outside Winchester, Virginia, the community of Gore was named for the Gore family and was the birthplace of Perry Cather Gore, the son for whom the Mosaic quilt was made. History records that this area changed hands seven times during the Civil War. The quiltmaker nursed both Confederate and Union soldiers during the course of that tragic conflict.

As an examination of her quilts reveals, Mrs. Gore was an accomplished artist, even by the high standards of southern needlework tradition. Her hospitality and generosity to guests extended even to passersby, as evidenced by a sign on the well near her apple orchard. Weary travelers were invited to partake freely of water and fruit. The *Virginia Quarterly* recounts that the Gores' "Valley Home" was the inspiration for the beloved lines by Sam Walter Foss, "Let me live in a house by the side of the road and be a friend to man."

The quilts were taken to Nowata, Oklahoma, in 1910 by Mrs. Gore's granddaughter, Lena Campbell Gore Burns. The present owner was reared from age three by Lena Burns, who was her step-grandmother.

MOSAIC WITH APPLIQUED FLORAL BORDER

Maker: Sidney Sophia Cather Gore (1828-1906). Made in Gore, Virginia, 1854.

Inscribed: "A wish for Perry: Oh! Had I but the magic power to rule thy destiny, I'd have thee know no sad'ning hour, No pang of misery. I'd have thee ever free from sin, As pure in heart as now. No darkened shadow e'er should fling its image o'er thy brow. Sidney"(in opposite corner)
"Presented to: Perry Cather Gore by his mother 1854."
"Remember thy creator in the days of thy youth"

Owner: Martha Burns Boren (Mrs. Horace C. Boren).

Pieced and appliqued: 97" x 84"; cotton: red, white and green; hand quilted.

See text, page 17.

18

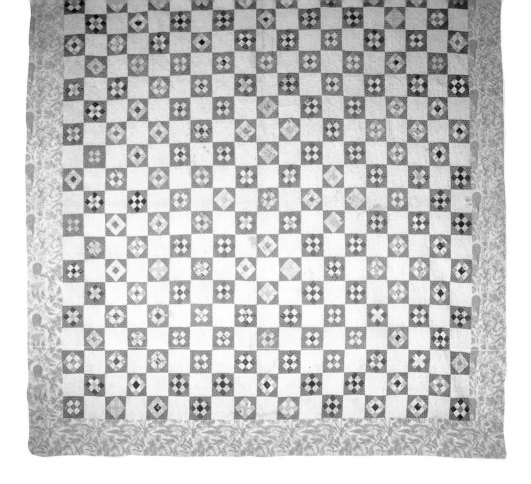

EMPRESS JOSEPHINE QUILT

Maker: **Origin unknown, 1771.**

Inscribed: **"1771" in satin stitch on the lining.**

Owner: **Roseanna Holstein Salm.**

Pieced: **101" x 100"; linen: French copperplate border and blue and brown on white; wool batting; hand quilted.**

By far, this is the oldest quilt registered in the Oklahoma Quilt Heritage project. It has a French copperplate border and pieced blocks made from finely woven linen. The year 1771 is embroidered on the lining and a history has been kept, with each owner recorded.

Records in the family's possession state that the quilt's first recipient was Empress Josephine, first wife of Napoleon Bonaparte; but there is no indication of who made the quilt. Josephine gave it to her lady-in-waiting, Martha Blar, who married a Mr. Miller and immigrated to New York. With her on the journey was her nurse, Rosina Haller, who later married a Mr. Stifal. When Mrs. Miller died in 1834, she left the quilt to Nurse Stifal. The Stifal family moved to Ohio and then to Illinois, but the "Empress Josephine quilt" was cherished as a very special heirloom.

There are 100 of the pieced blocks, each 4½" square. They alternate between a nine patch design and a square on point. The quilt top and lining are of fine woven linen. The border design shows a number of birds of various varieties, with hanging baskets amid a thicket of vines, grapes and berries. The quilting consists of many designs with fine, close stitches. Most of the rows are double and at no place are the rows over half an inch apart. The pieced blocks are quilted to follow the seams and the plain white blocks are quilted in five intricate designs: a star, flower, leaf, shell and square. The white lining is turned in a very narrow edge with back over the top to create the binding.

The condition is amazingly good, and the damaged portions are found in the nine patches where a brown print fabric was used.

OAK LEAF AND ACORN

Maker: Maria Gregg Israel (1838-1917). Made in West Virginia, circa 1858.

Owner: Catherine "Kay" Israel, granddaughter-in-law.

Applique: 90" x 89"; cotton: red and green on white; hand quilted.

Exquisite quilting stitches, fourteen to the inch, fill the background of this appliqued beauty from West Virginia. Made by Maria Gregg Israel when she was twenty, she gave it to her son, Emmett, when he left his native state for Oklahoma Territory to work on the railroads. He was a single man when he arrived in Keyes, Cimarron County, the most western county of Oklahoma; but he met Alma Schneider from Illinois and they married. The heirloom quilt became a wedding gift for the next generation and for forty-two years has been in the care of the present owner.

BASKET

Maker: Nancy M. Galloway (1843-1903). Made in Alabama, circa 1880.

Owner: Wanda McRee, great-granddaughter.

Pieced: 61" x 75"; cotton: red, green and blue; hand quilted.

During the 1800s it was not unusual for a quilt to be made wider than it was long so that it could cover not only the adults' bed but also the children's trundle bed which was pulled out at night. That may have been the case for this striking artifact.

Nancy Galloway's son, W.R. Galloway, remembered that his mother boiled green walnuts and various berries to make the dyes she used for fabric. The cotton batting in this quilt was hand carded. Nancy had eight children and this quilt came to Oklahoma Territory in 1906 with W.R. Galloway. He came by covered wagon from Texas to Stafford in Custer County due to the illness of his father-in-law, Robert L. Perryman, pastor of the Baptist Church of that community.

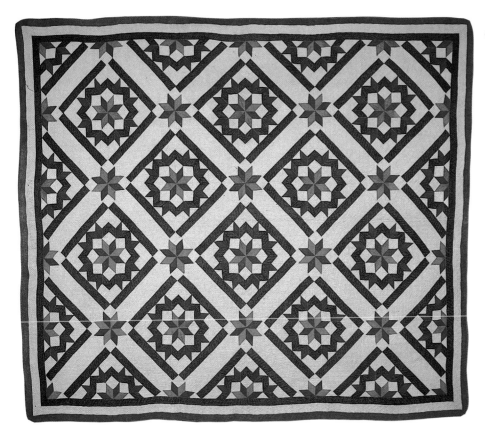

‹ CARPENTER'S WHEEL

Maker: **Sister of James Henry Shipp (possibly Sarah Voss). Made in Hart County, Kentucky, 1858.**

Inscribed: **"Sarah Voss," dated 1858, other initials.**

Owner: **Mrs. James R. Hankla, wife of great-nephew.**

Pieced: **95" x 82"; cotton: red, green, orange and white; hand quilted.**

Pieced by his invalid sister and quilted by relatives and friends, this quilt was presented to James Henry Shipp upon his enlistment in the Confederate Army. James served as a Captain in the Civil War.

During the battle of Vicksburg, Captain Shipp was hit with a spent ball, suffered sunstroke and was stacked with the dead. Fortunately he moved slightly and was pulled out by an observant soldier on burial duty. Family history records that fighting was so fierce and at such close range that Shipp saw powder burns as soldiers were struck. All night he heard the young men calling for their mothers. His descendants state, "He always grieved deeply because the soldiers were so young; and to him, the flower of the South died there."

The quilt was brought to Oklahoma by daughter Nannie Shipp Hankla and her husband when they settled at Geary, in Blaine County in 1909.

CRAZY QUILT **➤**

Maker: **Annie Elizabeth Stotts Sparks (1875-1953). Made in Adair County, Kentucky, 1895-1896.**

Inscribed: **Initials of maker plus sisters'.**

Owner: **Dorothy Trueblood Elliott, granddaughter.**

Pieced and embroidered: **88" x 73"; wool: variety of colors; not quilted.**

Annie Stotts made this quilt just prior to her marriage to Moses S. Sparks, on September 1, 1896, in Adair County, Kentucky. One of the animal designs was embroidered by her fiance'. Some of the pieces may have been done by her sisters whose initials are on the quilt along with her own.

The young couple came to settle in the Choctaw Nation of Indian Territory about 1899-1900 when the current owner's mother was a small child.

Moses and Annie Sparks

ORIGINAL FRUIT TREE DESIGN ❯

Maker: Elizabeth Jane Wray Jinkins (1830-1910). Made at Gibtown, Jack County, Texas, circa 1869-1896.

Inscribed: "G.R.E.L. Jinkins was born Jan. 30, 1869. This my son I done asking God to bless you when mother is gone."

Owner: Dorothy Ivester Patterson.

Appliqued, pieced, and embroidered: 62" x 81" cotton: yellow and red on white; hand quilted

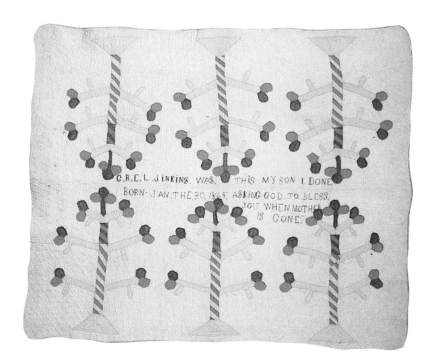

This charming Original Fruit Tree quilt, a design in naive folk art style, was made by Elizabeth Jinkins. A Missouri native and mother of fifteen children, Elizabeth made this quilt for her son Robert, who was referred to as "General." (It is assumed that the initials G.R.E.L. stand for General Robert E. Lee.) Though no records exist as to the exact year the quilt was made, it is believed to have been sometime between 1869 and 1896, the year of Robert's marriage to Susie Hitchcock in Jack County, Texas.

In 1899 the quiltmaker, by then a widow, journeyed to far western Oklahoma Territory to what is now Beckham County. There Elizabeth and a number of her sons and sons-in-law filed for land. "General" Robert Jinkins and his wife Susie were among those who filed.

MOSS ROSE

Maker: Mary Lindsey (1809-1858) and daughter Lydia Ann Lindsey Suratt (1834-1861). Made at Shiloh Plantation, McNary County, Tennessee, circa 1845.

Owner: Hazel Lucas Shaw, great-great-granddaughter.

Appliqued: 86" x 84"; cotton: red, green and white solids; wool batting; hand quilted.

Mary Lindsey and daughter Lydia Ann were assisted in the making of this quilt by slaves, referred to by the family as "household helpers." These trusted helpers were taught sewing and quilting and were proficient at "doing fine seams." Family history records that the Lindseys were loved by their slaves who refused to leave the family when freed.

In 1875 the Moss Rose quilt was taken to Montague County, Texas, via covered wagon by Lydia Suratt's newly married daughter, Rebecca Jane Suratt Worley. Rebecca and her husband moved to Edmond, in Oklahoma Territory, in 1892. The quilt has since passed through two generations.

ARROWHEAD

Maker: **Barbara Swartzendruber Stutzman (1849-1917). Made in Kalona, Iowa, circa 1900.**

Owner: **Mrs. W.C. Schantz, granddaughter.**

Pieced: **77" x 68"; cotton: blue and white; both hand and machine pieced; hand quilted.**

Mrs. Stutzman lived in the Amish community of Kalona, Iowa, when she made this quilt with its abundant cable and feather quilting designs. She gave it to one of her four children, daughter Catherine Johns, who came to Oklahoma Territory in 1905 and settled near Hydro in Blaine County.

DOUBLE HOURGLASS ❯

Maker: **Great-grandmother of Ruth Gerber. Made in Ohio, circa 1870.**

Owner: **Sheerar Museum, Stillwater, Oklahoma.**

Pieced: **75½ x 75½; cotton: brown, red, green and white; wool batting; hand quilted.**

When Ruth Gerber came to Stillwater, Oklahoma, in 1929 to join the faculty of Oklahoma A&M College (now Oklahoma State University), she brought with her this special quilt. It was a remembrance of her family in Ohio where her grandfather had served as a quartermaster during the Civil War. The quilt was stored in a trunk during the thirty-six years Dr. Gerber taught chemistry at the university before retiring in 1965.

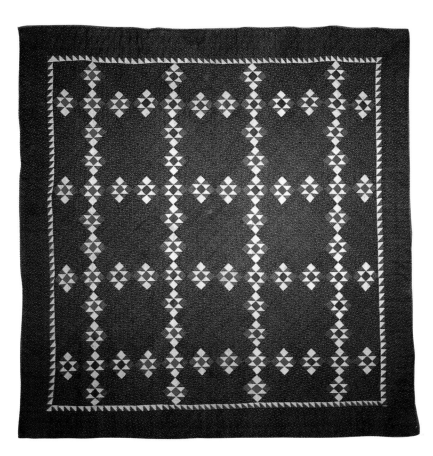

LOG CABIN, STREAK OF LIGHTNING ❯

Maker: **Serena Josephine Guy Carter (1843-1907). Made in Ardmore, Chickasaw Nation, Indian Territory, 1868.**

Owner: **Robert J. Perry.**

Pieced: **82" x 66"; cotton: red, white and tan (once green); wool batting; hand quilted.**

Serena Guy Carter made this Log Cabin quilt before the birth of her son, Charles D. Carter in 1868. Of Chickasaw descent, Mrs. Carter was then a resident of Ardmore, Indian Territory. Tribal custom at that period dictated that such quilts be retained by the recipient, and at his death be used to keep the body "warm" until burial.

Charles Carter's quilt remained with him, even in Virginia, where he resided during the twenty years of his tenure as the first United States Congressman from Carter County, Oklahoma. Charles married and was the father of four children, all of whom remained in the eastern United States. A daughter, Julia inherited Charles' Log Cabin quilt. The quilt, glass negatives of family photos and an array of family memorabilia were sold to a Virginia antiques dealer shortly before Julia's death in 1987. Fortunately, a brief note had been pinned to the quilt. Thus, the dealer, after research through genealogical records in Oklahoma, contacted Robert Perry, an avid researcher of Cherokee customs and the Trail of Tears. Perry's grandmother, Sophie (1887-1987) had been adopted and reared by Serena Carter, the quiltmaker. An orphan of Cherokee descent, Sophie was a distant relative of William R. Guy, the father of the quiltmaker.

The antiques dealer, though not interested in a cash transaction, ultimately traded the quilt and the glass negatives to Mr. Perry for pre-1890 Indian beadwork.

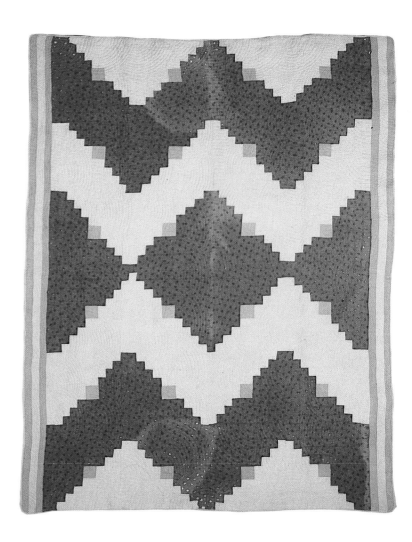

Serena Carter Guy

Chapter II

EARLY OKLAHOMA

A few of Oklahoma's early arrivals were wealthy and brought creature comforts with them, but most were young and had few worldly possessions. Early settlers arrived in a variety of conveyances, with covered wagons the most common mode of transportation. Travel was slow and large numbers of utility quilts were required for the journey. They were used to create beds and overnight, tent-like shelters. The first dwelling usually had only one room, so quilts created pallets on the floor at night and sometimes were hung to give the illusion of having two rooms. When time permitted, new utilitarian quilts were made; but gradually circumstances permitted the pioneer homemaker to make items that were not only useful, but added color and beauty to the home. Many of these early day Oklahoma quilts have been saved for the memories they evoke of bygone days.

The Oklahoma Star

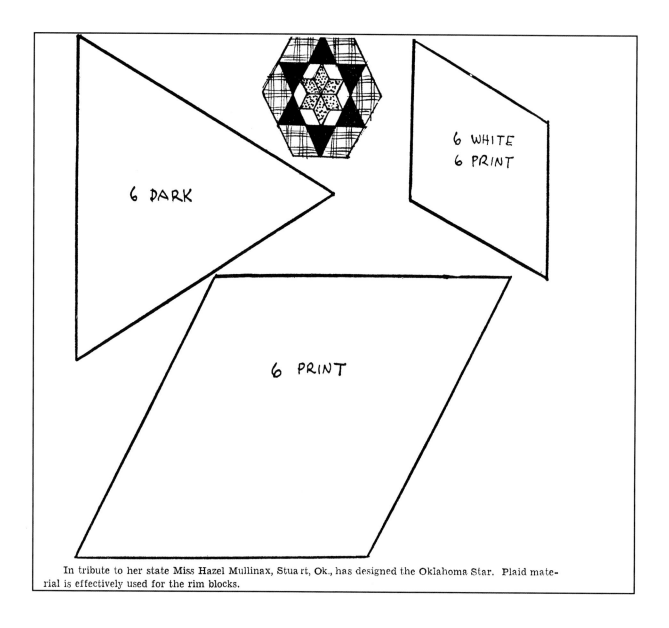

6 DARK

6 WHITE
6 PRINT

6 PRINT

In tribute to her state Miss Hazel Mullinax, Stuart, Ok., has designed the Oklahoma Star. Plaid material is effectively used for the rim blocks.

FLAT IRON ∨

Maker: **Minnie Fish Gigoux (c. 1866-1946). Made at Carrier, Garfield County, Oklahoma, 1920-1930.**

Owner: **Mrs. Lillian Gigoux, daughter-in-law.**

Pieced: **94" x 80"; cotton: red, white, yellow and blue prints and solids; not bound; hand quilted.**

    A native of Illinois, Minnie Fish at age 27 rode a horse sidesaddle in the Cherokee Strip Run, staking her claim two and one-half miles southeast of Carrier. A single man, J.P. Gigoux, staked the claim right across the road. The two later married and reared five children. The family lived on Minnie's land the first five years of the marriage, later moving to J.P.'s claim.

    Minnie Gigoux was known as an excellent seamstress and made many quilts. Family members have a photo of Minnie taken about the time of the 1893 Run. She is attired in a wool suit of her own design and wears a smart brown derby hat. Having enjoyed riding since her youth, Minnie purchased a horse with money earned as a seamstress.

Minnie Fish Gigoux

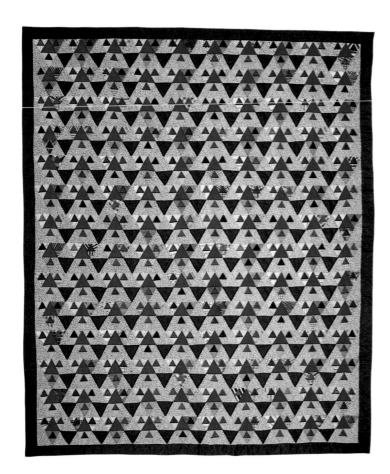

MISS JACKSON VARIATION >

Maker: **Elzora Mae Lyon Crusha (1885-1972). Made in Dewey County, Oklahoma, late 1930s.**

Owner: **Mrs. Ryan (Yvonne Merriman) Geddes, granddaughter.**

Pieced: **82" x 73"; cotton: variety of printed and solid scraps; tied.**

    Elzora Mae Lyon was born in Smith Center, Kansas, and like many others of her generation had little opportunity to attend school. Her formal education ended with third grade. At age ten Elzora came to Oklahoma Territory with her widowed mother to live with a married sister, Emma Lyon Hiler. The J.W. Hiler homestead was near Lenora in Dewey County.

The quiltmaker later married Albert Crusha and bore three children. In her lifetime she made numerous quilts, many of which were tied like this one rather than being quilted.

WINTER'S DREAM CRAZY QUILT

Makers: **Minnie Frances Witcher Anderson (1874-1964) and Leona Witcher Anderson (1868-1929). Made at McAlester, Pittsburg County, Oklahoma, 1915-1917.**

Owner: **Carolyn Grantham Wright, descendant.**

Pieced and embroidered: **74" x 55"; silk: multi colors; wool batting; hand quilted.**

The parents of quiltmakers Minnie and Leona Witcher were Elizabeth and John Witcher, who had traveled to the Choctaw Nation of Indian Territory before 1868. John Austin Witcher served as sheriff of Tobusky (Coal) County, the last Indian to have done so.

The sisters married brothers who were pure blood Chickasaw. The boys' parents, Ieachautubby and Aciah, had traveled via the Chickasaw Removal Trail to Peaceable Valley, south of McAlester, Oklahoma. Their sons, Joe and Hagen, attended missionary school, where they were forced to accept non-Indian names.

After they were married, the sisters lived only a mile apart. Leona was a seamstress and milliner, who often helped her sister Minnie with sewing for her five children. (Minnie also mended her sons' leather chaps.) Most of the sewing on the Winter's Dream Crazy Quilt was done on winter afternoons by the light of a coal oil lamp. The quilt is resplendent with symbols depicting the beauty of nature. Humor and whimsy have their place, as in the block with a mama frog holding hands with two baby frogs.

Minnie Francis Witcher Anderson

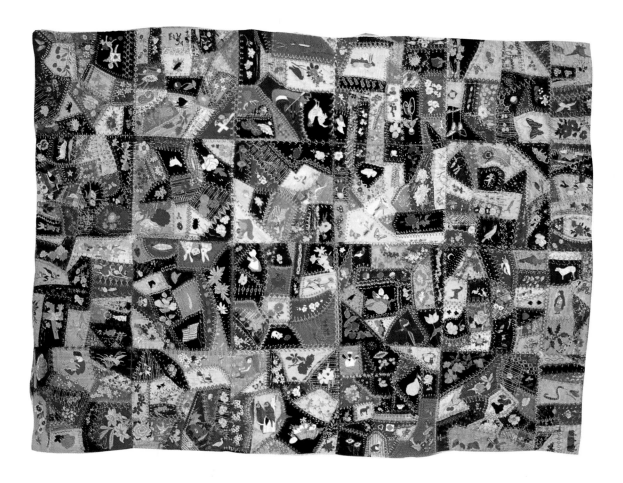

OCEAN WAVES ❭

Maker: **Essie Grounds Swaney (1863-1942). Made in Iowa and Illinois, 1875-1880.**

Owner: **Mrs. Margaret L. Hays, granddaughter.**

Pieced: **80" x 70"; cotton: a variety of printed and solid scraps; hand quilted.**

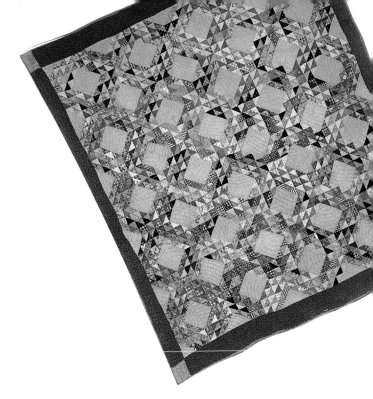

Essie Grounds Swaney and her husband went to Oklahoma Territory in 1894 with their five children. The family arrived by train, and Essie stayed in a hotel near the depot with the children while her husband located a place to settle. He first went to see a farm near Okarche but the land was too flat; he then went east of Oklahoma City and looked in Pottawatomie County but didn't find a place he liked. From the Meeker area he went east and then north and located a place he wanted near a settlement called Manila. The family of seven lived in a two-room cabin built on the banks of a creek running through the homestead. Soon after they settled in, a two story home was built north of the original cabin. They had four more children after coming to Oklahoma, and this quilt was in constant use until the late 1930's.

Essie Grounds Swaney

TULIP ❭

Maker: **Lydia Ann Spangler (born circa 1840). Made in Cherokee Nation, 1860s.**

Inscribed: **"the rina Bloom; maid in the Cherokee nation; maid by lydia a. Spangler . . honer the patern of the husbandary Remember me and this you see we will ceep hum ing"**

Owner: **State Museum of History, Oklahoma Historical Society.**

Pieced and appliqued: **83" x 72"; cotton: red, green, gold on white; hand quilted.**

When this Tulip quilt was given to Texas resident Lola Christopher in 1946, she knew little of her grandmother who made it. The quiltmaker, Lydia Ann Spangler, was half Cherokee and probably lived in the Papaw Bottom of the Arkansas River. Lydia gave the quilt to her son William Benjamin Spangler and taught him to appreciate his culture, thus throughout his lifetime he practiced many of the self-sufficiency skills of his ancestors. Affirming her family's Indian heritage, the quiltmaker's granddaughter presented the quilt to the Oklahoma Historical Society.

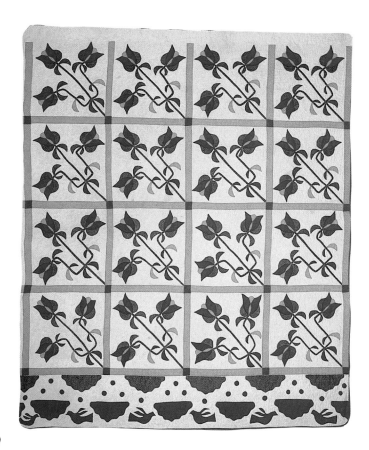

29

Gladys Key Perry

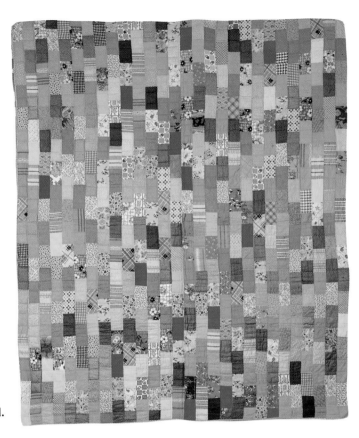

TRAVELING SALESMAN QUILT (Brick) ❯

Maker: **Gladys Key Perry (1911-). Quilted by Georgia Prater Watkins. Made at Goodwell, Texas County, Oklahoma, 1927.**

Owner: **Gladys Key Perry.**

Pieced: **80" x 68"; cotton: variety of prints and solids; hand quilted.**

J.D. Key, the father of quiltmaker Gladys Key Perry, made his first trip to No Man's Land (Oklahoma panhandle area) in 1906. He fell in love with the flat plains and bought a 160-acre homestead one mile north of the Texas line, due north of the present town of Booker, Texas. By the following year he had built a two-room house and broken sod to plant crops of barley, millet, corn, kafir and cane. In 1908, he married Gertie Day in Chandler and returned home by covered wagon, a trip of two weeks.

An enterprising businessman, Key built up a thriving freight-hauling business which contributed greatly to the growth of the area. Lumber for a larger home was purchased in Higgins, Texas, for $475.00 with all the hardware thrown in for free. The three Key children were born in that eight-room home which is still occupied. Their first telephone was connected by tying a wire along fence posts to LaKemp station two miles away.

The quiltmaker, daughter Gladys Key, started her first quilt for her dolls at age five, later completing it at age thirteen. This brick design quilt was made of swatches used by a traveling salesman. Swatches were shown to owners of general merchandise stores as samples; then orders were placed for the bolts desired.

Gladys moved with her family to Goodwell to attend high-school. She married in 1929 and reared three sons.

❮ SQUARE IN A SQUARE ORIGINAL SETTING

Maker: **Rebecca Price Proctor (birth date unknown - 1878). Made in Missouri, circa 1856.**

Owner: **Ruby Mason, granddaughter.**

Pieced: **78" x 70"; cotton: rose, teal and brown, home dyed with vegetable dyes; hand quilted.**

Though little is known of this quiltmaker, existing family documents reveal she resided in Arkansas and Missouri. While traveling with her family by covered wagon to Indian Territory in 1878, Rebecca Proctor died, leaving a daughter of sixteen months. This daughter was the mother of the quilt's present owner.

30

WHIG ROSE VARIATION (Also Harrison Rose)

Maker: Mary Ann Davis Wolfe (1827-1876). Made in Mecklenburg County, North Carolina, circa 1847.

Owner: Marguerite Anthony Grimsley, great-granddaughter.

Pieced and Appliqued: 84" x 78"; cotton: red, green, pink and gold on white; wool batting; hand quilt.

Mary Ann Wolfe presented this Whig Rose quilt to her daughter, Nola Wolfe Anthony, as a remembrance of her family when the Anthony family decided to "go west." The family traveled by rail to Wichita Falls, Texas, and settled in Archer County.

In 1901, the quilt was brought to Oklahoma Territory after the maker's son-in-law drew a land claim in the Kiowa and Comanche Territory lottery. The Anthony family settled near Gosnell (now Frederick) in Tillman County.

Brown circles visible along the center fold of the quilt occurred as a result of fording rivers during the trip into Oklahoma Territory. The boxes in which the quilts were packed became water-soaked, but this quilt was not unpacked until sometime after it was dry, rendering the water stains impossible to remove.

WHIG ROSE

Maker: Lydia Bailey Pybas (1846-1923). Probably made in Missouri, circa 1875-1900.

Owner: Lou Ann Pybas Hughes, great-granddaughter.

Appliqued: 80" x 76"; cotton: red, orange and green on white solid; hand quilted.

Quiltmaker Lydia Rice Bailey Pybas encountered tragedy and struggle during much of her early married life. First married just after the Civil War, she journeyed to Dexter, Texas, by covered wagon. Widowed in 1877, she was left with no money and four small children. She supported her hungry family by catching rabbits to eat and by selling fur-lined gloves made from the skins. When her sons were old enough to work, the family moved north to Indian Territory where Lydia worked as a cook and her sons as drovers at a cattle station.

There she met and married her second husband, J.C. Pybas. Seeking land of their own, the family homesteaded 160 acres when the Unassigned Lands of Oklahoma were opened for settlement. J.C. build a dugout for his wife, now mother of a baby son. The family still retains 75 acres of that homestead, located in what is now the Midwest City area, and the fifth generation of Lydia's family still resides on that property.

Maker: Alice Cochran Nichols (1875-1973) and her mother Almeda Killebrew Cochran (1849-1947). Probably made near Willis, Arkansas, circa 1890.

Owner: L. Pearl Henderson, daughter and granddaughter of makers.

Pieced: 77" x 60"; Linen and wool: linsey-woolsey; hand quilted.

Alice and her mother, Almeda, created this quilt in the true pioneer fashion. Their labor included raising sheep and shearing them with scissors, washing the wool, spinning, dying and weaving the fabric. For added strength in the fabric, they used linen threads from the poorer grade flax. The family called this homemade fabric "Lincy-wool" (sic).

Minnie Lehman Paxton

FEATHERED STAR WITH GARDEN MAZE SET >

Maker: Minnie Lehman Paxton (1873-1938). Made at Jester, Greer County, Oklahoma, circa 1930.

Owner: Ruth Suffridge, daughter.

Pieced: 92" x 77"; cotton: orange and red on white; hand quilted.

The quiltmaker, Minnie Lehman Paxton, was a native of Pennsylvania, but moved with her family to Texas before her marriage, eventually settling in Dallas. She was married there to Marshall G. Paxton in 1896, departing that same year for Greer County which had just become part of Oklahoma Territory, having formerly been considered part of Texas. The Paxtons filed for a homestead near Jester and built the dugout where three of their five children were born. Several years later a new home was built on the same farm where they homesteaded, and Minnie resided there until her death in 1938.

Minnie carded the cotton batting for the quilt from cotton grown on the family farm and quilted on a homemade quilting frame. Meticulous in sewing on her Minnesota Model A sewing machine, Mrs. Paxton sewed for her family, crocheted, embroidered and made about a dozen quilts.

SIX-POINTED STAR

Maker: Sarah Foster McGranahan. Made at Oklahoma Station (now Oklahoma City), Oklahoma, circa 1888.

Owner: Robert and Aimee' Treece, great-great grandson.

Pieced: 76" x 67"; cotton: brown, gold, red, maroon; hand quilted.

Sarah Foster McGranahan and husband James arrived at Oklahoma Station, now Oklahoma City, around 1887. For two hundred fifty dollars they purchased a house and business located west and north of what is now the Santa Fe railroad station. At that time there were five wooden buildings, several tents and a population of about fifty people. The railroad had reached there the previous year. James took over as agent for the stage line, and soon after became postmaster. Sarah was feeding and housing mule-skinners and others in their two story building called the ARBEKA Hotel, which means in the Creek Indian language, "plenty to eat."

Sarah McGranahan and her mother, Mrs. Margaret Foster, made this quilt while Sarah was living at Oklahoma Station.

MRS. DEWEY'S CHOICE ➤

Maker: Sarah Foster McGranahan. Made at Oklahoma Station (now Oklahoma City), Oklahoma, circa 1888.

Owner: Sharron Treece Tinsley, great-great-granddaughter.

Pieced: 78" x 74"; cotton: blue, white, red and yellow, some are dyed tobacco sacks; hand quilted.

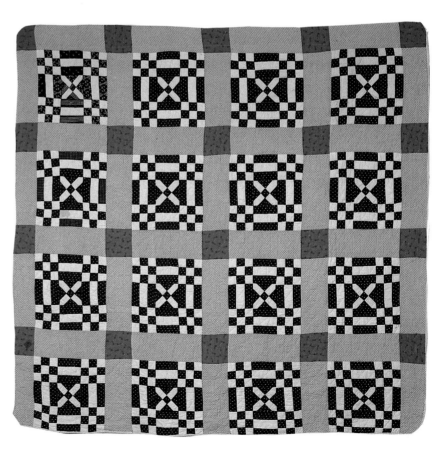

33

NINE-POINTED LONE STAR

Maker: **Rosina Bader Hawks (1840-1918). Made at Hennessey, Kingfisher County, Oklahoma, 1913.**

Inscribed: **"Mother Age 73 Xmas 1913"**

Owners: **George W. and Norma Hawks, grandson and wife.**

Pieced: **86" x 86"; cotton: red, blue and gold on white; hand quilted.**

The quiltmaker's husband, John S. Hawks, staked a claim in the Unassigned Lands Run, April 22, 1889, and the family arrived from Ohio on June 1. Later he served as circuit-rider minister for the Congregational Church in the Territory and founded the Congregational Church in Carrier, Oklahoma.

Holding down a town lot. Guthrie, OK. April, 1889.
Oklahoma Historical Society photo.

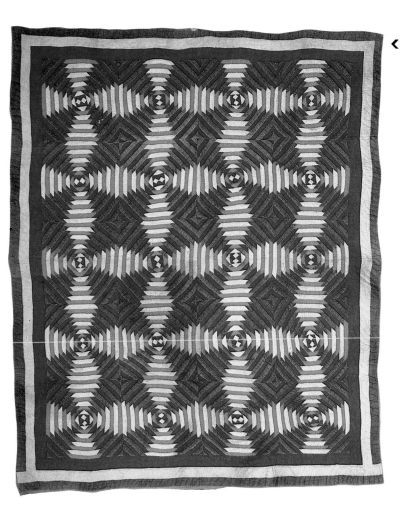

PINEAPPLE

Maker: **Elizabeth Airington Barnett (1854-1937). Made at Ada, Pontotoc County, Oklahoma, 1923.**

Owner: **Helen W. Armstrong Crabtree, granddaughter-in-law.**

Pieced: **81" x 66"; cotton: red, blue, gold and white; hand quilted.**

The mother of quiltmaker Elizabeth Barnett had walked at age eight to Indian Territory during the Choctaw Removal. Born in the Choctaw Nation in 1854, Elizabeth was married to Archibald J.S. Barnett at age fifteen in a ceremony uniting several couples - a Choctaw custom at that time.

Elizabeth Airington Barnett

GRANDMOTHER'S FLOWER GARDEN, MINIATURE

Maker: **Cordelia Jones Freeman (1879-1970). Made in Wilburton, Oklahoma, 1934-1935.**

Owner: **Grace Freeman Moore, daughter.**

Pieced: **89" x 76"; cotton: variety of colored prints set with pale blue solid; hand quilted.**

At age ten Cordelia Jones watched her father, E.B. Jones, astride a horse with red saddle blanket, make the Run for a stake in the Unassigned Lands of Oklahoma Territory. On April 22, 1889, he staked his claim at what is now Norman, Oklahoma. In 1900 Cordelia married David Hood Freeman, settled in the mining community of Krebs, Oklahoma.

This masterpiece of craftsmanship contains a collection of scraps from home sewing. Cordelia fashioned 15,616 dime-sized hexagons into the two hundred fifty-six blocks comprising this quilt.

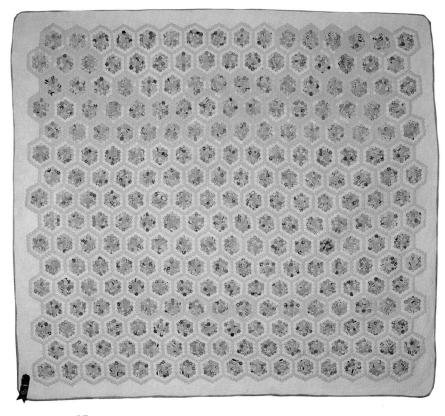

35

◀ COXCOMB VARIATION

Maker: **Member of Schmidt family. Made in Ripley County, Indiana, circa 1850.**

Owner: **Mabel A. Steele, descendant.**

Appliqued: **87" x 86"; cotton: red, pink, green and white solids; hand quilted.**

Applique technique at its best is found in this graphic quilt made in Indiana. Although the name of the quiltmaker is not known, the Schmidts were a family of excellent quilters; and the quilt is thought to have been made by a niece of the owner's great-grandmother, Elizabeth Schmidt Westrup.

Elizabeth was married in 1863 to John Frederick Westrup and after seven years the family moved from Indiana to Abilene, Kansas. Thereafter the quilt passed to daughter Sophia Elizabeth Westrup Cammerer, who with her husband Albert William homesteaded in Woodward County, Oklahoma Territory, in 1895.

EAGLE QUILT ▶

Maker: **Mary McElwain Chenoweth (1815-1897). Made in Webster County, Missouri, 1860. Quilted in 1900 by Nancy Elizabeth Palmer Chenoweth and daughters-in-law Cora King Chenoweth and Rosanna King Chenoweth.**

Inscribed: **"Presented to Benjamin Franklin Chenoweth by his Mother, 1860"**

Owner: **Maude Chenoweth Leaman, great-granddaughter.**

Appliqued and pieced: **75" x 73½" cotton: red, green and gold on white; hand quilted.**

Born in Clinton County, Ohio, Mary McElwain moved westward with her parents and in 1832 married Luke Chenoweth in Indiana. As new areas opened, Luke Chenoweth, like his ancestors, moved west to find land and a home for his family. After building a log home in Iowa, Luke died at age thirty-nine, leaving his young wife Mary with six children and a large farm to maintain. Mary's three youngest sons served in the Civil War. In 1889 these three made the run into the Unassigned Lands of Oklahoma Territory, bringing their wives and the Eagle Quilt top with them. In 1900 the top was quilted by Benjamin's wife, Nancy Elizabeth, with her two daughters-in-law.

Through the years the quilt has been in the possession of the eldest relative.

Chapter III

QUILTING STORIES

Fortunately, many families passed the story of the quilt along with the artifact. Often the owner was too young to have ever known the quiltmaker personally, but had been told things by the previous generation that made the person seem real--how the quilting frame was lowered from the ceiling when in use, how field cotton was cleaned, carded and batts made, the favorite chair of the quiltmaker for piecing, and perhaps most important of all, the joy the quiltmaker had in her creation. Quilts have been called "love stitches" and were a common way of expressing love and caring.

The Oklahoma Wonder

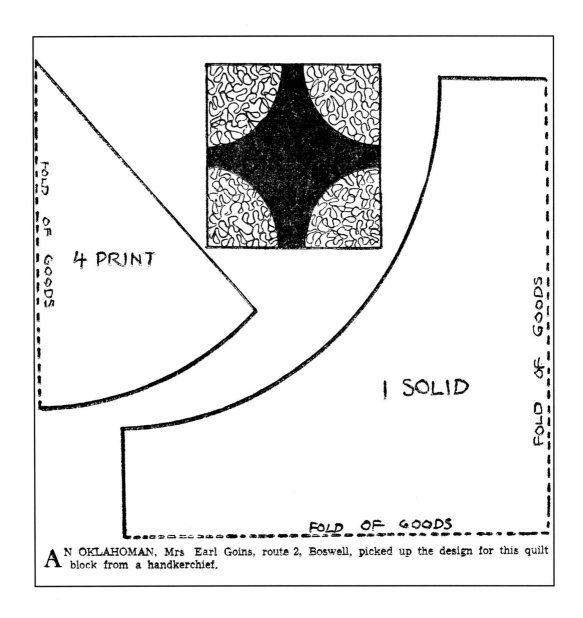

FOLD OF GOODS

4 PRINT

FOLD OF GOODS

1 SOLID

FOLD OF GOODS

AN OKLAHOMAN, Mrs Earl Goins, route 2, Boswell, picked up the design for this quilt block from a handkerchief.

RAINBOW CACTUS

Maker: **Verlinda Standridge Goodner (c. 1878-1938). Made at Edmond, Oklahoma County, Oklahoma, 1935-1936.**

Owner: **Ruth Goodner King, granddaughter.**

Pieced: **86" x 70"; cotton: variety of scrap prints plus rose, green and white solids; hand quilted.**

Made by Verlinda Goodner for her granddaughter's hope chest, this Rainbow Cactus quilt is a classic example of 1930s quiltmaking. The favorite rose and green color scheme set with scraps is characteristic of the period. Confined to a homemade wheelchair by rheumatoid arthritis, Mrs. Goodner worked at a quilt frame hung from the ceiling in a cold west room. Granddaughter Ruth King has many memories of this quilt, as she was then living with her grandparents while attending Central State Teacher's College (now University). She worked for her room and board which was a common practice for those privileged with the opportunity for higher education during the Depression years. The quilt was later proudly displayed at Ruth's wedding in May of 1938.

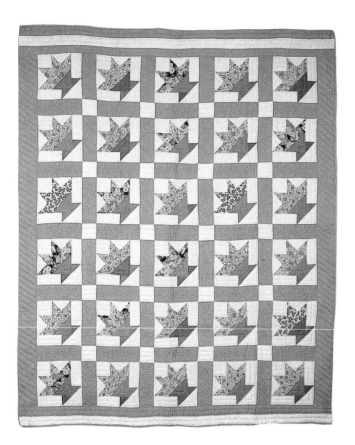

Tabitha Taylor Shaffer

ROAD TO OKLAHOMA ❯

Maker: **Tabitha Taylor Shaffer (1856-1937). Quilted with her daughter, Natola Shaffer Lamar. Made at Coyle, Logan County, Oklahoma, 1933.**

Inscribed: **"Mother Age 77 1933"**

Owner: **Gloria Helen Lamar, granddaughter.**

Pieced: **88" x 82"; cotton: rose and white solids; hand quilted.**

Tabitha Taylor Shaffer designed and executed many quilts during her lifetime. After having presented each of her sons with a quilt, she determined to create for her son-in-law, Albert Leonard Lamar, a quilt with a setting unlike any she had previously tried. For this very special quilt she selected the "Road to Oklahoma" block, set 16 of the blocks on point to form a central medallion, and let the remaining four blocks "float" on point near the quilt's corners. The design is framed by an unusual broken strip border.

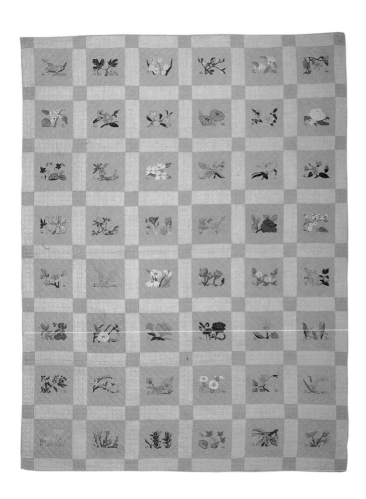

EMBROIDERED STATE FLOWERS

Maker: Mary E. Ittner Clark (1894-   ). Made at Glencoe, Payne County, Oklahoma, 1936-1939.

Owner: Mary E. "Lizzie" Clark.

Embroidered and pieced: 90" x 70"; cotton: beige and yellow with colorful crewel embroidery; hand quilted.

Some artists use paint, others clay or wood, but Mary "Lizzie" Clark created beauty with needle and thread. The pattern was from a newspaper and her sister, Viola, furnished the material and thread for two quilts to be made simultaneously, one for each of them.

As a small child, Mary traveled with her grandparents, parents, uncle and two sisters in a covered wagon from Sedgwick County, Kansas, to a farm in Indian Territory. The family's first home was a dugout.

SPIDER WEB >

Maker: Hattie Campbell Wheeless (1878-1978). Made at Olustee, Jackson County, Oklahoma, late 1930s.

Owner: Blanche Olson, daughter.

Pieced: 86" x 68"; cotton: variety of scrap prints and solids; hand quilted.

Using scraps from the many dresses, shirts and suits she made for her six children, Hattie Wheeless created this graphic rendition of an old traditional quilt pattern. Having traveled to Oklahoma by covered wagon in 1916, the Wheeless family saw many hardships, but by hard work and good management insured that their children were well clothed and fed. This pioneer work ethic is typical of the hardy settlers who have populated Oklahoma from territorial days to the present.

40

FIELD OF DIAMONDS IN BARS　　➤

Maker: Mrs. Eastwood (c. 1847-1938). Quilted by the Worthwhile Club of Wilson. Made at Ada, Pontotoc County, Oklahoma, circa 1920s.

Owner: Sylvia Hennigan.

Pieced: 81" x 64"; cotton: print scraps; sateen lining; hand quilted except one row of machine stitches at each end to stabilize.

The unique setting of this Field of Diamonds quilt gives it the appearance of a folding screen. The source of this setting is unknown, but is thought to have been an original idea of Mrs. Eastwood, who pieced the top.

The top was quilted in the late 1930s by Sylvia Hennigan and members of the Worthwhile Club of Wilson, an active service club of twelve members. The group made quilts for needy families and for those who lost their homes and belongings in house fires.

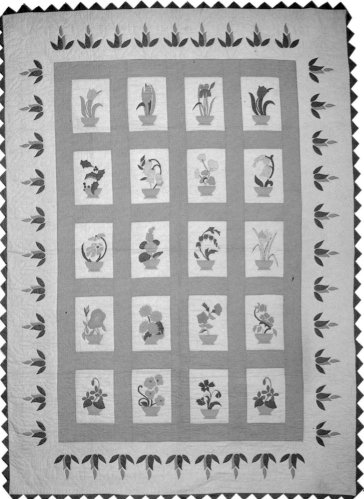

❮　　MEMORY BOUQUET

Maker: Ethel Smith Breeding (c. 1880-1975). Quilted by her sister, Elsie Smith Edwards. Made at Sand Springs, Tulsa County, Oklahoma, 1930-1932.

Owner: Katherine Skalnik Winslow, granddaughter.

Appliqued and pieced: 102" x 75"; cotton: green and multi-hues; prairie point border; hand quilted.

Quilting was extremely popular during the 1930s, and thereafter interest in this art waned for several decades. Ethel Breeding, born in Kansas and resident of Sand Springs from her young adult years on, followed this trend. The lovely Memory Bouquet quilt pictured here was one of only three quilts that she made during her lifetime. The pattern source for this quilt was the *Kansas City Star* and her fabric was probably purchased especially for this quilt with the exception of the flowers which could have been scraps left from many garments she made for her family.

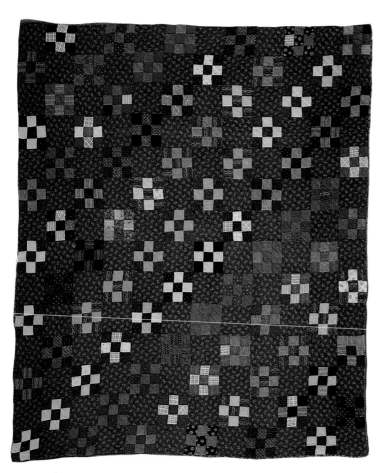

❮ NINE PATCH

Maker: Sallie Seay Cabe (1872-1968). Made at Westville, Adair County, Oklahoma, 1907.

Owner: Mrs. Charles Gruenberg, granddaughter.

Pieced: 76" x 64"; cotton: variety of scraps set with indigo print; hand quilted.

Sallie Seay spent the first part of her life in Arkansas. By 1907 the decision was made to move to Westville, Adair County, Oklahoma, for the children's educational opportunities. She had eight children and they made their home on a farm in eastern Oklahoma.

In many ways, her life story is typical and this Nine Patch quilt is typical of quilt patterns and fabrics of the era.

Sallie Seay Cabe

DUTCH TILE ❯

Maker: Mattie Green James (1877-1968). Made at Ravia, Johnston County, Oklahoma, circa 1938.

Owner: Obera James Cypert, granddaughter.

Pieced: 70" x 60"; cotton: variety of scraps in blue and red prints set with yellow; hand quilted.

Mattie Green James was a Tennessee native who moved to Arkansas with her family and later into Indian Territory in 1881. Mattie was the mother of two sons and she reared granddaughter Obera, the present owner of the Dutch Tile quilt.

The quiltmaker's family recalls that Mattie was a prolific quiltmaker, having completed approximately 150 quilts. Though she did all the work on each quilt herself, she enjoyed visiting the neighbors while she hand pieced her quilt blocks. Her effective use of striped fabric gives a most contemporary feel to her design.

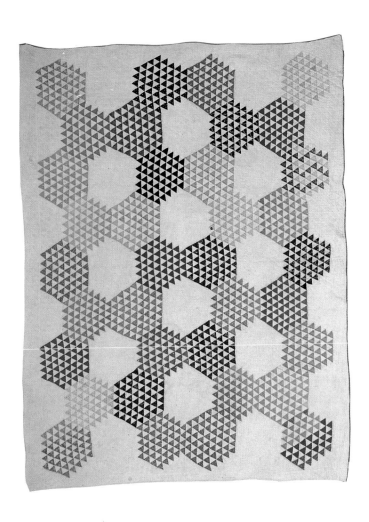

TRIANGLE MOSAIC VARIATION

Maker: **Mary Jo Ewing Ott (1858-1935). Quilted with sister, Susan Ewing Morton (1844-1915). Made in Kansas or Oklahoma, circa 1885.**

Owner: **Galada W. Jantz, granddaughter.**

Pieced: **82" x 62"; cotton: scraps, mostly reds and flour sacks; hand quilted.**

The Ewing sisters did superb crosshatch quilting on this scrap quilt which includes the use of white flour sacks. Mary Jo Ewing made many quilts, and as she had nine children, no doubt many were needed in their Ames, Oklahoma, farm home. This Triangle Mosaic was used only as a bedspread, so the granddaughter who received it knows it had special significance to the maker.

ORIGINAL BARS ❯

Maker: **Gladys Johnson Poynor (1900-1986). Made in Tulsa, Oklahoma, circa 1920-1930.**

Owner: **Gulia Peggy Poynor Foster, daughter.**

Pieced: **68" x 66"; cotton: blue and white; hand quilted.**

Finding new ways to arrange simple, traditional blocks to achieve a totally different look has been a perpetual challenge for quilters. Quiltmaker Gladys Poynor set two-patch and four-patch blocks alternately with white in vertical rows separated by wide blue bars. The result--a quilt with a decidedly contemporary look.

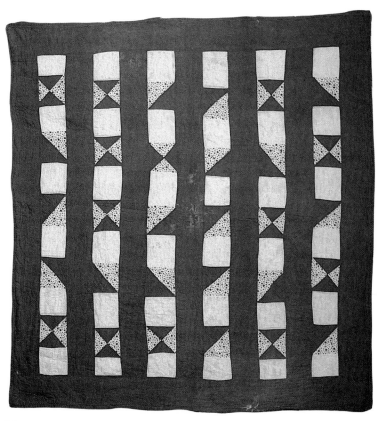

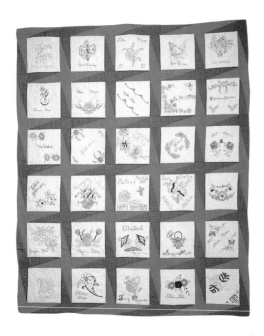

FRIENDSHIP FLOWER

Maker: Ines Smith (1895-1973). Quilted by Maggie Smith (1871-1960). Made at Vici, Dewey County, Oklahoma, 1939.

Owner: Irene Randall, daughter.

Pieced and embroidered: 85" x 70"; cotton: white blocks with pink and green setting; hand quilted.

Ines Smith made hundreds of quilts for her family of twelve children but this one has special memories for her daughter Irene for whom it was made. She recalls that her mother started it as a surprise gift for her eighteenth birthday. Irene was a student at Vici High School at the time and when the top was complete, Irene's grandmother, Maggie Smith, added to the gift by doing the quilting.

The striking contrast of color and design of the sashing sets off the floral blocks and adds movement across the entire quilt surface.

DRESDEN PLATE ▶

Makers: Ladies of First Baptist Church Missionary Society. Quilted by Ethel Raines (1887-1970). Made at Grove, Delaware County, Oklahoma, 1933.

Owner: Anna B. Hedges Graham.

Pieced and appliqued: 92" x 74"; cotton: green and pink; hand quilted.

In the Depression years, fund raising was a major concern and women's church groups spent many hours creating quilts to make ends meet. This quilt from the Grove community exemplifies a common method. The ladies sold spaces for names at 10¢ each and their names were embroidered on the block.

When the top was complete, a widow, Mrs. Ethel Raines, did the quilting on a free-standing frame in the dining room of her home. A young teacher was rooming with Mrs. raines that year and remembers watching the progress each day. To add more dollars to the church treasury, the completed quilt was purchased by a church member. Mrs. Noah Harrison, for $25.00.

About 1973, some of Mrs. Harrison's quilts were being sold; and, sight unseen, the current owner agreed to buy one. The person making the sales arrangements could not have known that the quilt selected would be one that Mrs. Graham had watched being made when she was the first-year teacher rooming with Ethel Raines.

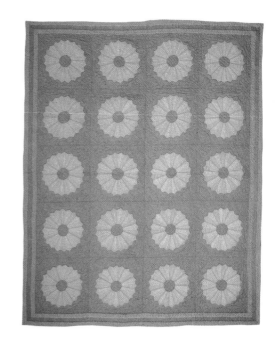

◀ COLONIAL DAYS

Maker: Emma Quinn Yaeger (1872-1946). Made at Duncan, Stephens County, Oklahoma, circa 1928.

Owner: Emma Lou Provine, granddaughter.

Pieced and embroidered: 72" x 59½" cotton: pink and white; hand quilted.

Blue-eyed Emma Quinn Yaeger was of Irish descent. She was born and married in Georgia and at age twenty came by train with her husband to a farm they purchased near Duncan in Indian Territory. They lived on the farm for 54 years and her namesake granddaughter, Emma Lou, remembers going there for many wonderful visits. The quiltmaker's sister and daughter lived with her and they all enjoyed quilting. Frequently, neighbors came by to join them at the quilting frame which was hoisted to the ceiling of the dining room when not in use.

Mrs. Yaeger made many quilts, including two from this pattern which was printed in *The Daily Oklahoman* newspaper in 1926. This quilt was made for Emma Lou and the other for her brother, John Harrison.

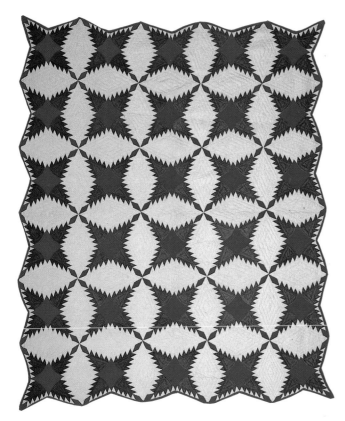

PINE BURR

Maker: Nancy Ellen "Mollie" Ward Shellenberger (1855-1937). Made in Love County, Oklahoma, circa 1910.

Owner: Leta Faye Forbes Wilkins, granddaughter.

Pieced: 83" x 68½"; cotton: red, green and white solids; hand quilted.

"Mollie" Shellenberger

Mother of 14 children, "Mollie" Shellenberger was widowed in 1905. She pieced numerous quilts, many after losing the sight in one eye. Many quilt patterns used by the quiltmaker were clipped from the weekly *Kansas City Star*.

Most of the last twenty years of the quiltmaker's life were spent north of Marietta, Oklahoma, in the home of her daughter, Cora Shellenberger Forbes. Mother and daughter quilted together, and Cora's husband raised the cotton which was hand carded for quilt batting. The present owner was one of seven granddaughters in the home and recalls the quilt frame suspended from the ceiling. Though most family quilts were made from scraps, "Mollie's" Pine Burr quilt was made from fabric purchased especially for this purpose.

Mary Casey Craig

CHEROKEE SEVEN STAR ❯

Maker: Mary Casey Craig (1891-   ) Made at Savanna, Pittsburg County, Oklahoma, 1937.

Owner: Jewell Craig Glover, daughter.

Pieced: 78" x 63"; cotton: green, yellow and red on white; hand quilted.

Quiltmakers have always modified patterns to solve a design problem or to incorporate symbols and ideas of their own. An excellent example is this adaptation of the "Seven Sisters" block. Quiltmaker Mary Craig took a traditional block she liked and set it within a Cherokee Star which has tiny triangles pointing outward from a circle. The quiltmaker's daughter relates that her father was of Cherokee descent and loved their symbols. Thus evolved the Cherokee Seven Star quilt.

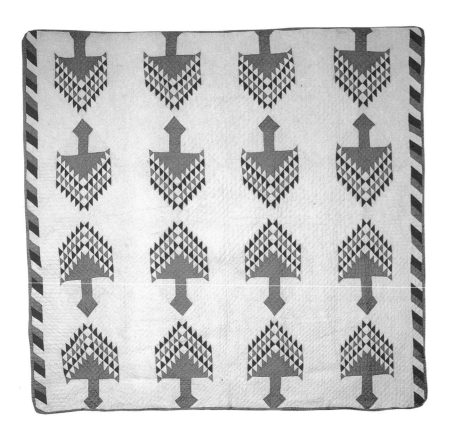

TREE OF PARADISE

Maker: **Lola Lee Watkins (1878-1953). Made at Boswell, Choctaw County, 1930s.**

Owner: **Mary Watkins Allen, daughter.**

Pieced: **82" x 78"; cotton: red, green and white: hand quilted.**

Described by her family as quite talented in handwork, Lola Lee Watkins pieced many quilts and preferred working on challenging pieced blocks rather than applique. Her stunning Tree of Paradise showcases her ability handsomely.

Desiring her standards of quilting excellence to be carried on in her family, Mrs. Watkins began her daughter's instruction in the art at age ten.

ROCKY ROAD TO KANSAS >

Maker: **Cynthia Ann Williams Richey (1868-1928). Made in Scottsville, Kentucky, circa 1886.**

Owner: **Cora Richey Cassady, daughter.**

Pieced: **80" x 69"; cotton: red, blue, green (faded) and white; hand quilted.**

This stunning quilt with its graphic sashing contains blocks constructed by the "string piecing" method. Maker Cynthia Ann Williams Richey was a Kentucky quilter who grew her own cotton for spinning into thread, weaving of cloth and carding of her quilt batts. Seeds for her four rows of cotton were sent to her by a brother in Oklahoma. Mrs. Richey earned money for the purchase of calico by selling sugar cakes for ten cents each.

In October of 1928 Mrs. Richey journeyed by train to Oklahoma for a family visit, bringing eight of her quilts with her. She died there just two months later.

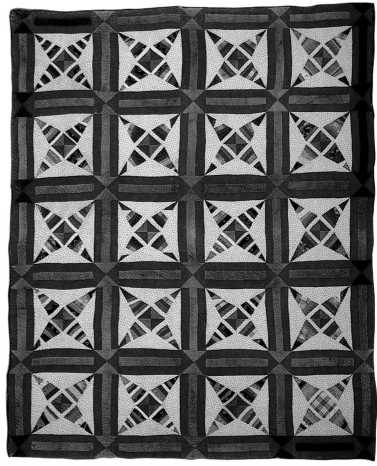

TRIP AROUND THE WORLD

Maker: **Gladys Rush Jones (1889-1939). Quilted by maker, Gladys Jones and Lena Rush. Made in Oklahoma City, Oklahoma, 1932.**

Owner: **Juliet Johnstone Sharp, niece.**

Pieced: **82" x 66"; cotton: six tints of rose solid; hand quilted.**

When Gladys Jones and her three sisters reached adulthood, Gladys embarked upon a challenging project: creating a Trip Around the World quilt for herself and one for each of her three sisters. She decided to make each quilt in a different color, and in due time decided upon rose, blue, yellow and lavender. Each quilt required six tints of the color, but this was no problem as her husband J.C. was an associate of C.R. Anthony, founder of the Oklahoma department store chain of the same name. Gladys thus had access to a large selection of piece goods.
Her mother and one of her sisters helped with the quilting and the first completed was this one in rose, made for the birth of her sister, Mae Rush Johnstone, mother of the present owner.

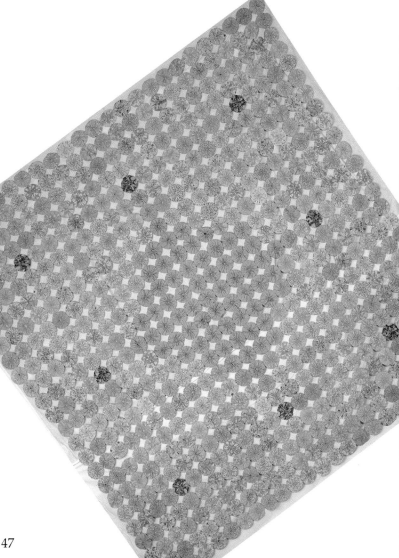

YO-YO MEDALLION DESIGN ❯

Maker: **Beatrice Vineyard Linscott (1879-1962). Made at Atoka, Atoka County, Oklahoma, 1920s.**

Owner: **Elaine Chappel, granddaughter.**

Yo-yos: **86" x 82"; cotton: pastels and green; no quilting.**

Yo-yos are not truly quilts for they have no batting, backing or stitches to hold the layers together. These novelty "quilts" were very popular in Oklahoma during the 1920s and 1930s and were used as bedspreads. Children were often given scraps of fabric to make into yo-yos as a means of learning to sew and to keep them entertained.
Most yo-yo spreads were made from assorted scraps and no particular plan appears in the arrangement of colors. This example made by Beatrice Linscott uses sixty-six green yo-yos in the center to form a design.

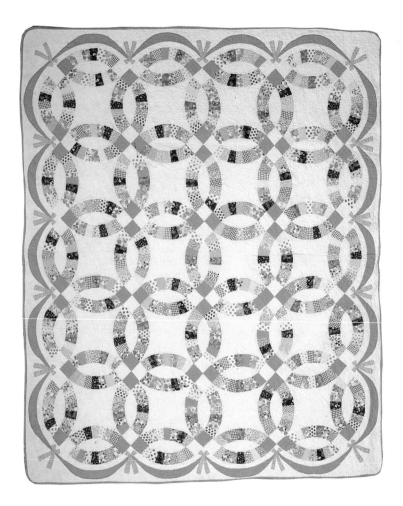

DOUBLE WEDDING RING

Maker: **Arminda Lucinda Cooper Estelle (1864-1956). Made near Arcadia, Oklahoma County, Oklahoma, 1930s.**

Owner: **Colleen Keyes Sarani, great-great-granddaughter.**

Pieced and appliqued: **88" x 72"; cotton: multi prints with green solid on white; hand quilted.**

Of English descent, Arminda Cooper married and came to Oklahoma Territory just three years after the area was opened for settlement. The family lived on a farm in the Arcadia area and she made many quilts, twenty of which are still in existence. Arminda quilted regularly during the 1920s and 1930s with a group of friends.

The next person in Arminda's lineage to become a quilter was a great-great-granddaughter and in the 1980s she obtained this Double Wedding Ring quilt and an unfinished top. She took the quilt top back to the area where it had been made fifty years previously and some of the friends with whom Arminda had quilted so many years ago completed the item.

SUNBURST ❯

Maker: **Lillie Mae Graumann Frank (1915-   ). Made at Granite, Greer County, Oklahoma, 1932.**

Owner: **Lillie Mae Graumann Frank.**

Pieced: **87" x 70"; cotton: coral and white; hand quilted.**

Precise machine piecing is the hallmark of this quilt and the maker recorded in her own words how she learned to sew on a sewing machine. "As a small child I held a passionate fascination for the sewing machine. When my mother would go outdoors to care for the chickens or do various chores, I would quickly sneak to the sewing machine to pedal that treadle and watch the needle sew. I would often use a sheet of tablet paper and run the threadless needle along every line. That is how I learned to sew a straight line."

Lillie Mae made this Sunburst quilt when she was home following high school graduation. She had learned to quilt as a young child in the 1920s. Each winter her mother made a quilt or two with all the children assisting and her husband offering words of encouragement. Lillie Mae writes, "During these times and into the Depression era of the early thirties, cash was a scarce commodity. This necessitated every savings possible. Therefore we would not purchase cotton batting but would use cotton from our own farm. We planted it, chopped it, cultivated it, and picked it. At the gin, mother asked the workers to keep some of the cotton out of the bale. She then took this to a mattress factory in Hobart to be made into batting."

She concludes, "What a good feeling it was, to be so self-sufficient. And often our delight was elevated while we were stitching a quilt with the aromas of bread baking in the kerosene oven, or of soup made from ingredients that we had raised or made. We seemed to have a sense of security even in times of economic depression, dust storms and few entertainment devices, largely due to our family togetherness and creativity ventures. Our church and faith meant much, too."

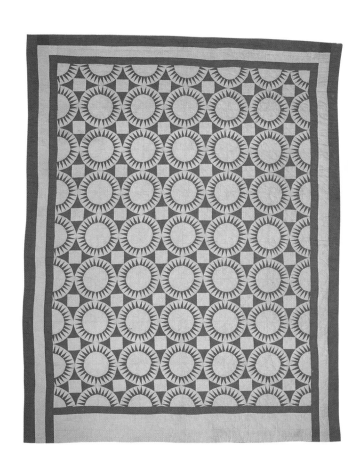

NEW YORK BEAUTY

Maker: **Member of the Linder family. Made at Gallespy, Alabama, circa 1875.**

Owner: **Mrs. Emmit B. Hedrick, great-granddaughter of original owner.**

Pieced: **78" x 69"; cotton: red, green and gold solids on white; hand quilted.**

Presented to Helen Elizabeth Turner Milam on the occasion of her wedding, this meticulously rendered New York Beauty quilt was brought to Oklahoma around 1895. Its original owner stipulated that it was always to be left to a descendant named "Helen". Representing the sixth generation of her family since the quilt was made, its present owner, Helen Hedrick, inherited it from her great-aunt, Helen Pearl Hileman.

SUNBURST 〉

Maker: **Ethel Alma Watson McCollum (1884-1967). Made at Helena, Alfalfa County, Oklahoma, circa 1935.**

Owner: **Ruth Ann McCollum, granddaughter.**

Pieced: **85½" x 73"; cotton: blue and yellow; hand pieced.**

Though many sunburst type quilts were registered in Oklahoma, this example by quiltmaker Ethel McCollum deserves a second look both for its uncommon color scheme and for the original set or placement of the sunburst blocks. Add to Ethel's originality her mastery of quilting and hand piecing, and the result is an heirloom to treasure.

Born in Missouri to Drury and Mary Frances Watson, she married Charles Edward McCollum in 1903. They were the parents of six children.

Esther Blalack Naylor

ROCKY ROAD TO KANSAS

Maker: **Esther Marie Blalack Naylor (1926-). Quilted by Artie Beall Hulsey Blalack. Made at Wilburton, Latimer County, Oklahoma, 1939.**

Owner: **Esther Marie Blalack Naylor.**

Pieced: **81" x 73"; cotton: variety of scrap prints and solids set with orange; hand quilted.**

Esther Naylor was taught at age eight to use the sewing machine. At age thirteen she made this quilt. First using a cardboard template to trace pattern shapes onto newspaper, she then sewed fabric strips to the paper by machine. After the paper pattern was covered, the excess fabric was trimmed off along the edges of the paper. When the blocks were assembled and the quilt top completed, the paper backing was torn away.

This method, called "string piecing" or "strip piecing" was in common use even in frontier days. It was one method to construct a quilt quickly and was especially favored for construction of utility quilts – those which were for everyday use. In addition, this method provided a means for using even small scraps and therefore was commonly used by children learning to sew before they were given large pieces of fabric.

ORIGINAL YO-YO BASKETS >

Maker: **Celia Gertrude Adams (1889-1988). Made at Sapulpa, Creek County, Oklahoma, 1930s.**

Pieced and appliqued: **98" x 83"; cotton: multi-prints on white; hand quilted.**

This atypical design top with pieced back creates a truly reversible quilt. The quiltmaker filled her free form baskets with flowers fashioned from yo-yos which were in vogue as a needlework technique during the 1930s. A nice collection of period fabrics forms the bars on the front of the quilt and its binding. One is surprised to turn it over and see a totally different design and style on the quilt back.

A quilt, by definition, must consist of three layers: a top, a batting, and a back; and these must be held together with stitches. The stitches that hold this Yo-Yo Basket quilt together are exquisite and while it is not known how many quilts Celia Adams may have done previously, these stitches were made by a skilled needle artist.

50

◄ **PRAIRIE POINTS IN A CIRCLE** (Target or "Quill")

Maker: Ora Robertson Baughier (1880-19049). Made at Decatur, Texas, early 1900s.

Owner: Jennifer D. Mayer, great-granddaughter.

Folded triangles: 79" x 72"; cotton: variety of scraps and feedsacks.

Born in Booneville, Mississippi, of Dutch ancestry, Ora Baughier was a quiet, retiring lady dedicated solely to her family. She did not do crochet or fancywork, preferring instead to sew useful articles for her family. She utilized clothing scraps and feed sacks to fashion the thousands of folded "prairie points" which comprise this piece.

According to Karoline Bresenhan and Nancy Puentes, co-authors of *Lone Stars: A Legacy of Texas Quilts, 1836-1936,* Target or "Quill" quilts, of which Mrs. Baughier's is but a single example, originated in the southern states or with quiltmakers who emigrated from that area. Therefore, this type of novelty quilt may be considered a true regional quilt style.

HEXAGON STAR WITH FLOWERS ➤

Maker: Mary Watkins Allen (1910-   ). Made at Boswell, Choctaw County, Oklahoma, 1930.

Owner: Mary Watkins Allen.

Pieced and appliqued: 90" x 80"; cotton: prints on orange with green and purple; hand quilted.

Mothers and daughters do not always see eye to eye when it comes to choosing colors. This Hexagon Star quilt was made while Mary was in high school. She recalls that her "Mother nearly went into shock" when Mary brought home orange and purple fabric to finish the quilt. It seems she got tired of piecing small hexagon flowers and decided to do something else rather than making the entire quilt surface of small hexagon shapes. The quiltmaker indicates that piecing and making quilts was her form of entertainment in those years.

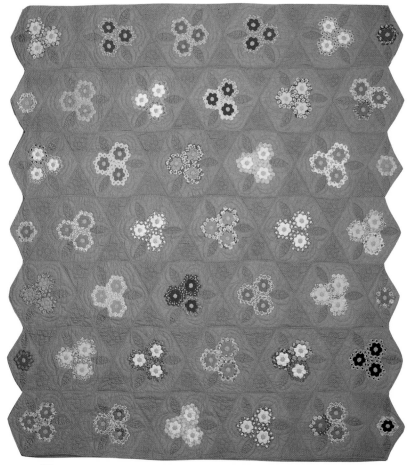

WHIG'S DEFEAT 1871, WHIG'S DEFEAT 1930, and PINE BURR 1931 ❯

Maker: Martha Mills Brown (1848-1939). 1871 quilt made at Marshall, Arkansas, and others made at Weatherford, Custer County, Oklahoma.

Owner: Mary Nelle Shults Hutto, granddaughter.

Pieced and appliqued: Whig's Defeat 1871, 92" x 69"; cotton: orange, green and white. Whig's Defeat 1930, 90" x 69"; cotton: orange, red, green and white. Pine Burr 1931, 85" x 71", cotton: blue and white. All three quilts are hand quilted.

Martha Mills Brown's childhood included family tragedy related to the Civil War. Born in Georgia to Caleb and Malvina Lawrence Mills, her family started on a journey by wagon to Arkansas at the start of the war. A band of renegades stopped them, burned her father's feet, and then shot him. Her sister, Hester Mills, went to her father's rescue, was shot and died after ten days. Mrs. Mills and her remaining children finally got to Arkansas.

Martha later married and had three children. She was never content to sit with her hands idle. The 1871 quilt was made when she was a young woman in her twenties. In 1910 she and her husband moved to Oklahoma to be near their daughters and in 1930 after she was widowed, she pieced the Whig's Defeat pattern again, this time in orange, green and red.

Complex patterns were a readily accepted challenge and at age 83, Mrs. Brown made the blue and white Pine Burr quilt with beautiful feathered quilting designs. In the last years of her life when she could no longer quilt, her daughter bought thread for her to use in tatting, for even then she was not satisfied to be idle.

Whig's Defeat, 1871

Whig's Defeat, 1930

Martha Mills Brown

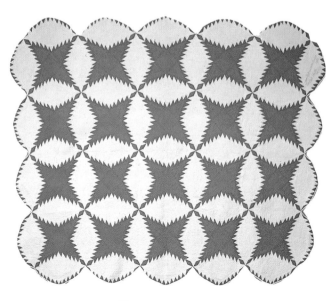

Pine Burr, 1931

APPLIQUED BUNNIES ➤

Maker: Marie Hampel Turner (1906-1976). Made at Enid, Garfield County, Oklahoma, circa 1936.

Owner: Rita Turner Carter, daughter.

Appliqued: 49" x 34"; cotton: rose and white solids; hand quilted.

Meticulous workmanship and exquisite hand quilting make this charming baby quilt an heirloom to cherish. Bunny quilts were popular in the 1930s, and this quilt probably was made from a published design. The quiltmaker's daughter found paper tracings of the bunnies in an envelope with a 1936 postmark, leading to supposition that perhaps a friend had shared the pattern.

The quilt is in excellent condition, having never been used. It is not known for whom the quilt was made.

GOLDEN WEDDING RING ⌄

Maker: Elizabeth Crawford (1891-1986). Made in Tulsa, Oklahoma, 1937.

Owner: Jenni Orvis Roswurm, great-granddaughter.

Pieced: 74" x 65"; cotton: variety of scraps with blue faded to purple and white; hand quilted.

1906 was a special year for quiltmaker Elizabeth Crawford: her family joined others to form a wagon train from Illinois to Indian Territory. She met her husband-to-be on that trip. Though she was just fifteen, they were married later that same year.

In 1937, by then a resident of Tulsa, Elizabeth used a pattern designed by her mother-in-law, Frances Emiline Crawford, to make matching quilts for her grandsons. The boys, Roger and Bruce Orvis, grew up with the quilts, and Bruce's daughter Jenni is the proud owner of one of the matching pair.

Elizabeth Crawford

STAR OF TEXAS and ORIGINAL DESIGN

Maker: **Lola Oxendine Johnstone Murray (1882-1955). Made at Bartlesville, Washington County, Oklahoma 1931 and 1932-1933.**

Owners: **Mrs. Charles R. Johnstone, daughter-in-law (Star) and Mary Frances Murray Haas, daughter (Original).**

Pieced: **88" x 84" (Star) and 78" x 76" (Original); cotton: variety of pastel solids and red; hand quilted.**

During the 1930s, the concept of "make it do" and avoiding waste was one that permeated all of society. Delightful, original adaptations came about because of the basic precept that no fabric should be discarded.

Lola Murray wanted to make a special quilt to be given as a wedding gift to her son Charles and his bride Myrtle. She cut the diamond pieces too large and the design would not go together. Putting those units aside, she started over again, cut more fabric into the proper size, assembled and quilted the Star of Texas for the 1931 wedding.

The first, oversize units were then creatively assembled into a new, original design, and a quilt was made for her daughter, Mary Frances.

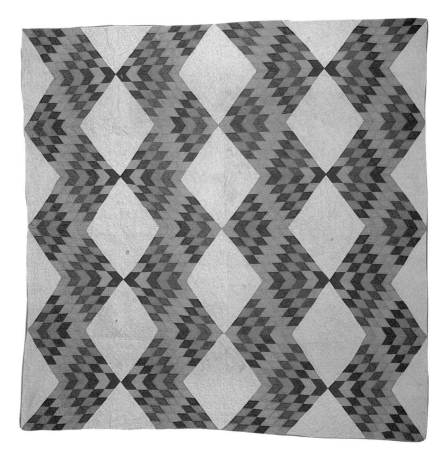

54

BROKEN STAR VARIATION

Maker: Bessie Shields Marple (1891-1982). Made at Bartlesville, Washington County, Oklahoma, circa 1930s.

Owner: Mrs. Wayne Marple, daughter-in-law.

Pieced: 86" x 78"; cotton: rainbow hues on white; hand quilted.

A native of Kansas, Bessie and her husband, Gus Marple, owned and operated a grocery store in Bartlesville for fifty years. She was an excellent seamstress and won numerous honors at local fairs for her handwork. Bessie's granddaughter notes that, "She could not understand written patterns, but would say 'just let me look at the piece'."

LIVE OAK TREE

Maker: Bessie Shields Marple (1891-1982). Made at Bartlesville, Washington County, Oklahoma, circa 1930s.

Owner: Sheri Lynn Marple Brown, granddaughter.

Pieced: 95" x 80"; cotton: blue on white; hand quilted.

Among quiltmakers, tree patterns have been popular through the decades. This Live Oak Tree design is seldom seen and like so many other tree motifs requires intricate, accurate piecing to be successful. Bessie Marple evidently made a variety of quilts in the 1930s but for this one she used blue and white fabric in the blocks from the turn of the century. One can imagine the fabric might well have been saved from a previous generation's dressmaking remnants.

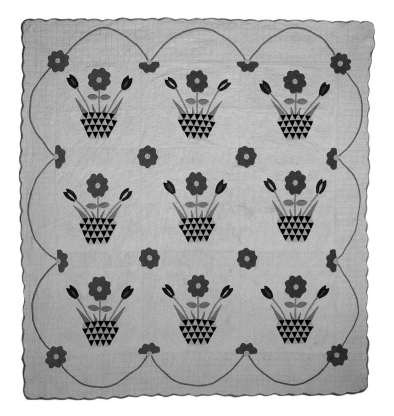

SPRINGTIME

Maker: Rohesa Anne Harmon Elrod (1867-1949). Made at Lovell, Logan County, Oklahoma, early 1930s.

Owner: Dorothy Jeanne McLaughlin Resneder, granddaughter.

Appliqued and pieced: 80" x 77"; cotton: red, blue, yellow and black on white; hand quilted.

Meticulous workmanship and fine hand quilting enhance this quilt in naive folk art style. Rohesa Elrod was an avid quilter, as her diaries confirm. She attended quilting bees in Lovell and was never known to decline an invitation from a friend with a quilt in the frame. Always a social outlet, quilting was also her solace after the death of her husband in 1928.

Rohesa Harmon Elrod

ROSE TREE WITH WATERMELON BORDER ❯

Maker: Sarah Elizabeth Kirkwood White (1890-1979); Made at Belleville, Arkansas, 1932.

Owner: Rebecca White Jones.

Appliqued: 90" x 82"; cotton: rose, yellow and green on white; trapunto on "love apples"; hand quilted.

Sarah Elizabeth Kirkwood White, a prolific quiltmaker with hundreds of quilts to her credit, won numerous prizes and awards for her work. This stunning Rose Tree quilt with its tasseled watermelon border was created in Arkansas in 1932. The design, not original with the quiltmaker, exemplifies applique motifs and colors typical of thirties quilts. In addition to meticulous applique work and quilting, Mrs. White exhibits a skill for trapunto, or stuffed work, on the oval "love apple" (bud-like) motifs.

1930s Fair sponsored by Shawnee Indian Agency.
Oklahoma Historical Society photo.

56

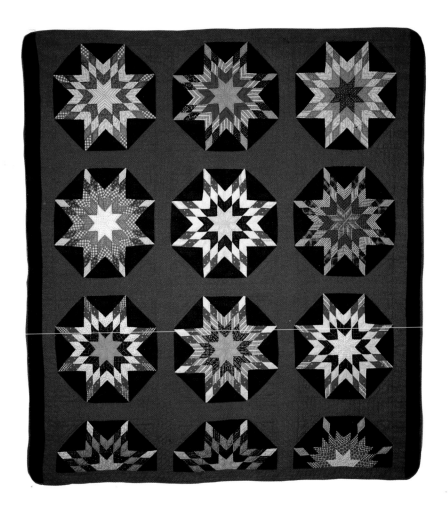

BLAZING STAR OF KENTUCKY

Maker: Minnie Roberts Mitchell (1884-1963). Made at Valliant, McCurtain County, Oklahoma, 1918-1920.

Owner: Edith Mitchell Powell, daughter.

Pieced: 84" x 76"; cotton: printed shirtings plus red, blue and white solids; hand quilted.

Minnie Mitchell's daughter recalls, "Mother picked the cotton from their farm, took it to the gin and then carded the cotton into batts. She had nine children and therefore did much quilting at night by kerosene lamp light.

"Our only heat was from the fireplace, and we hardly had room to get before the fireplace because a quilt was always in the frame in that room. At that time we didn't appreciate it, but now we children love to scan the quilts for scraps from our clothing.

"Mother got most of her patterns from the *Kansas City Star*. She used bark from walnut and other trees to dye fabric for her quilt linings."

Minnie Roberts Mitchell

MOSAIC >

Maker: **Martha Whitfield Rhodes (1822-1910). Made at Griggsville, Illinois, circa 1900.**

Owner: **Carolyn Camp Foster, great-granddaughter.**

Pieced: **79" x 70"; cotton: variety of scraps in prints and solids; hand quilted.**

Martha Whitfield Rhodes was born in Wakefield, England, and as a girl of thirteen was sent to a "Girl's School of Industry." While a student there, she perfected her skills in all forms of hand sewing and needlework.

In 1848 the Rhodes family emigrated to America, eventually settling in Illinois in 1856. Martha's skills and energy did not diminish with the years, as evidenced by the Mosaic quilt shown, whose pieces are no larger than a postage stamp.

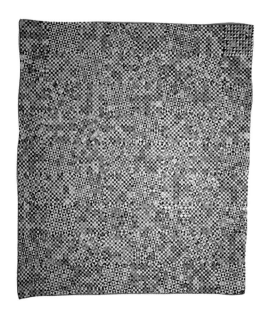

❮ NINE PATCH

Maker: **Dorothy Winkler Kamphaus (1917-   ). Made at Canute, Washita County, Oklahoma, 1939.**

Owner: **Dorothy Winkler Kamphaus.**

Pieced: **85½" x 74"; cotton: variety of scraps plus red and white; hand quilted.**

Quiltmaker Dorothy Kamphaus started quilting as a teen-ager and completed this Nine Patch with its unusual set and sawtooth borders when she was twenty-two. The mother of seven children, Mrs. Kamphaus is a descendant of a family of quiltmakers. She states, " . . . my mother and neighbor ladies had quilting bees in their homes and I helped make quilts for our church bazaar. My grandmother made quilts and I had always admired her talent."

CRAZY QUILT >

Maker: **Mary Ann McCann Crosby (1851-1920). Made at Bixby, Tulsa County, Oklahoma, 1912-1917.**

Owners: **Helen Boles and Roberta Edwards, great-granddaughters.**

Pieced: **82" x 65"; cotton and wool: scraps in a variety of colors; an abundant use of embroidery, including Indian motifs not quilted.**

The quiltmaker's father was from County Cork, Ireland, and her mother was a full-blood Creek Indian. Her family states, "Even after she was partially paralyzed at age 65, she would walk to church—or at least start—if someone didn't come after her."

Her initials are on this cotton and wool quilt, along with a large variety of Indian designs and thread work.

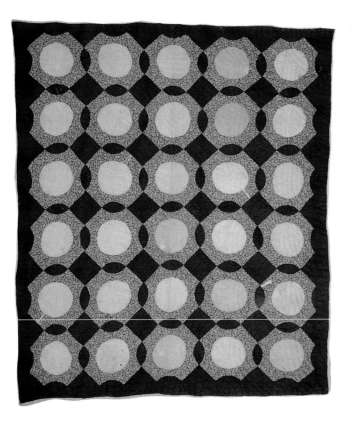

FULL MOON

Maker: **Etta Mouser Coleman (1877-1956). Made near Pickens, Pushmataha County, Oklahoma, circa 1930.**

Owner: **Fayrene Ferguson Benson.**

Pieced: **76" x 66"; cotton: turquoise print, purple solid and white; hand quilted.**

This 1930s quilt of the "snowball" type employs a seldom seen pattern published in the *Kansas City Star.* The quiltmaker, Etta Coleman, was an Arkansas native who later came to Indian Territory with her parents. She was married in 1892 in what is now Leflore County, and bore eleven children.

By the time this quilt was pieced Mrs. Coleman was legally blind, yet she managed to continue piecing quilts by "feel."

Etta Mouser Coleman

DOUBLE WEDDING RING ❯

Maker: **Clara Eva Frame Allen (1879-1960). Made at Ketchum, Delaware County, Oklahoma, circa 1930s.**

Owner: **Norma Jeane Hensley.**

Pieced: **82" x 68" cotton: reds and scraps; hand quilted.**

Double Wedding Ring was one of the most favored quilt patterns in the 1930s. Perhaps its popularity stems from the romantic name but more likely it is because one could use tiny scraps to make a beautiful design. Most were set together with white but the exhuberant red fabric used by Clara Allen makes the scraps in the arcs sing. She made many quilts and the *Kansas City Star* was her major pattern source. Like so many quilters, her frame was hung from the living room ceiling to make it handy yet get it out of the way when not in use. She quilted for about sixty of the eighty-one years she lived.

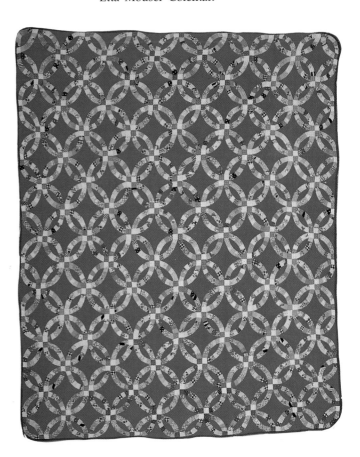

PINWHEEL

Maker: Zagonyi Litzenberger Nonnamaker (1861-1951). Made near Warren, Ohio, 1906-1911.

Inscribed: Initials in corner.

Owner: Pauline Griebel Hamilton, granddaughter.

Pieced: 86" x 72½"; cotton: scrap prints and white solid; hand quilted.

Zagonyi Litzenberger was born in Peoria, Indiana, in a small cottage near the home of her grandparents, operators of a gristmill there. Called "Gonia", she was named for Colonel Zagonyi, an army officer, a common practice during the Civil War era. Gonia married Franklin Nonnamker in 1888 and bore seven children. After residing in Indiana and Kansas, the family settled permanently in Ponca City, Oklahoma, in 1917.

The Pinwheel quilt was stitched with love and sorrow, chiefly from scraps and from fabric of an unworn dress of a daughter, Evalyn, who died of pneumonia in 1905 at the age of nine.

Imogene Dennis Roberts

TWIN STAR HEXAGON　❯

Maker: Imogene Dennis Roberts (1889-1941). Made in Pawhuska, Osage County, Oklahoma, circa 1935.

Owner: J. Margaret Roberts, daughter.

Pieced: 86" x 76"; cotton: red, green, gold, lavendar and white; hand quilted.

When the popularity of quilting reached its 1930s zenith, Imogene Dennis Roberts was one of its most outspoken advocates.

As president of the Pawhuska DAR chapter, Imogene Dennis Roberts organized a quilt show. Some quotes from newspaper articles reporting the event reveal her attitude toward quilting: "A few years back scarcely a woman in this city had more than a passing acquaintance with the subject of quilts and quilting. Today patchwork quilts with their sharp angles and startling color contrasts are monopolizing the attention of Pawhuska women and bringing about a revival of the craft which boasts such a romantic history . . . For the first time in the centuries that have elapsed since an Egyptian cut figures from a goat skin and created the first primitive "quilt," this form of woman's handwork is becoming recognized for its true worth. There is real art in making pieced and appliqued quilts while the quilting is another art in itself . . . No amount of time or effort is too great for the woman who has succumbed to the lure of quilts."

Prior to her 1921 marriage, Mrs. Roberts taught Latin, Spanish and English and served as Dean of Women at a state teacher's college in North Dakota. For her own quilts she chose very old traditional patterns rather than the "new trendy patterns like Double Wedding Ring, Grandmother's Flower Garden and French Bouquet." She loved quilting and Twin Star Hexagon proves her skill with twelve tiny stitches per inch. She also quilted tops for other women of the town and usually was paid $1.25 per spool. In 1939 she was shocked to be paid the high some of $60.00 for quilting a pair of twin size quilts.

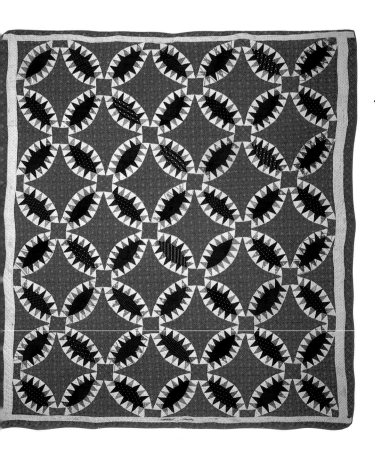

PICKLE DISH

Makers: America Murphy (c. 1833-1913) and sister "Sis" Fuller, Made at Walter Hill, Tennessee, 1912.

Owners: Hildreth Charlton (original owner) and Boothe Charlton Millspaugh, daughter.

Pieced: 76" x 70"; cotton: red, white, dark blue and light blue; hand quilted.

Purchased from the makers, who made and sold quilts, this vibrant Pickle Dish quilt was given as a wedding gift to Howard and Hildreth Charlton in 1912.

Prior to 1910 Howard had traveled from Tennessee to Oklahoma on foot, paying his way by selling Bibles. When he had sufficient funds he rode the train for a distance. Eventually settling in Hollis, Oklahoma, in 1910, he soon married and in 1913 opened his own business, The Hollis Dry Goods Store.

DRUNKARD'S PATH VARIATION

Maker: Lettisha Reno Lewis (1841-1918). Made in Pattonsburg, Missouri, 1880s.

Owner: Nella Gentis Short, granddaughter.

Pieced: 86" x 70"; cotton: variety of red and blue prints on white solid; hand quilted.

Born in Hardin County, Kentucky, Lettisha Reno was married at age 16 to James Lewis in Illinois. The couple moved to Pattonsburg, Missouri, where most of their nine children were born. Near the turn of the century the family moved to a farm near Lucien in Noble County, Oklahoma Territory.

Lettisha used feed sacks for the backing of her quilt. The setting of this Drunkard's Path is unusual because of the use of two extra four-patch blocks horizontally in addition to the four blocks which make the basic "X" pattern.

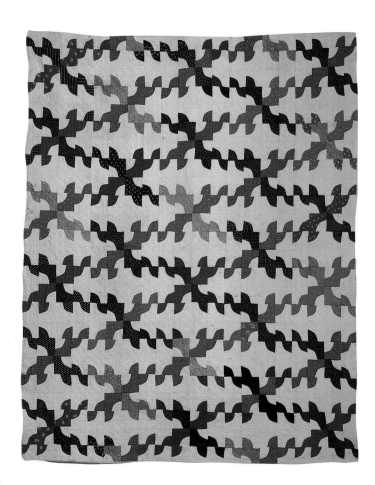

61

Dugout. "A modest home in Oklahoma 1896." Oklahoma Historical Society photo.

ONE DOZEN TULIPS   ∧

Maker: **Lela Johnson Walter (1893-1981). Made in Alden, Caddo County, Oklahoma, 1938.**

Owner: **Lahoma Butler Rackley, niece.**

Appliqued and pieced: **91" x 77"; cotton: red, yellow and green on white; hand quilted.**

Sharing of patterns among friends and between one generation and another in a family is an old custom with quilters. This pattern was sent to Lela Johnson Walter in 1924 by her mother-in-law, Effie Mae White Walter, who lived in Nebraska. Four quilts were made in Oklahoma using this pattern.

Lela was born in Illinois and came to Oklahoma Territory around 1901 in a covered wagon with her parents. When the family first arrived in southwestern Oklahoma, they lived in a dugout located thirteen miles south of Carnegie.

Lela Johnson Walter

62

Chapter IV

DAILY LIVING

The quilt, of all the household items, was most apt to have been made by the family that used it. Hence, it seems logical that it tells a great deal about daily living. Names of the quilt patterns spoke of commonplace items like "Broken Dish," "Church Dash" or "Goose In the Pond." Milestones in lives were exemplified by pattern names and by the receiving of a quilt as a gift for a new baby, school graduation, wedding or a special birthday. Life encompasses joy and sorrow, birth and death; and the family quilts reflect this cycle.

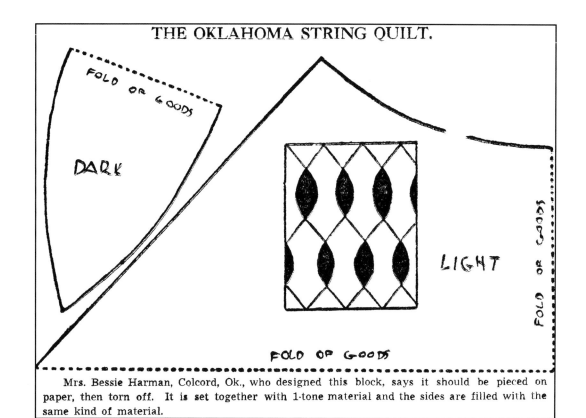

THE OKLAHOMA STRING QUILT.

FOLD OR GOODS

DARK

LIGHT

FOLD OR GOODS

FOLD OF GOODS

Mrs. Bessie Harman, Colcord, Ok., who designed this block, says it should be pieced on paper, then torn off. It is set together with 1-tone material and the sides are filled with the same kind of material.

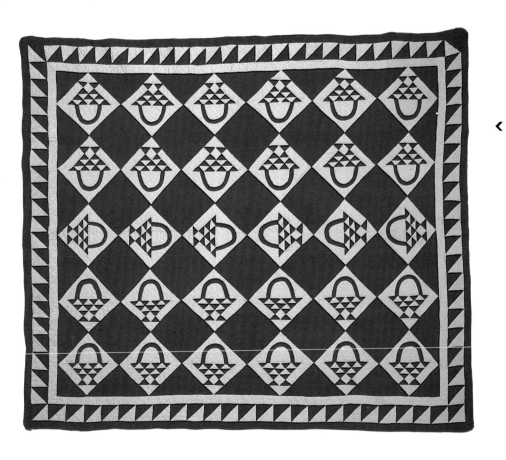

FLOWER BASKET

Maker: Ella Sherman Nevins (1877-1914); Made at Minneola, Kansas, circa 1900.

Owner: Joyce M. Fischer, granddaughter.

Pieced: 80½" x 68"; cotton: red and white; hand quilted.

Ella Sherman married Lewis A. Nevins at Minneola, Kansas, on November 3, 1895. She died around 1912 giving birth to their seventh child. Five years later when the family moved to Oklahoma, the quilt came with them.

STYLIZED TULIP WITH CURRANTS

Maker: Margaret Rebecca Singleton Rose Brooksher (1843-1924). Made in Tennessee, 1861.

Owner: Mrs. Ethel Foster, granddaughter.

Appliqued: 83" x 82"; cotton: red, green and yellow on white; hand quilted.

At age eighteen, Margaret Rose was a young wife whose husband was away fighting in the Civil War. She put countless hours into this quilt, appliqueing the unique top design and then quilting it in triple rows. Her husband was killed in the war leaving behind a small son. Family tradition says that President Lincoln intervened on behalf of the young widow and protected her from enemy soldiers.

Later she married again, and bore seven children. The family came to Oklahoma Territory in 1900 where James Brooksher was a farmer and rancher in Caddo County. In 1913, he rented a railroad car and moved his cattle and possessions to Tahlequah. Their new farm consisted of 110 acres on the Illinois River.

Through war and moves halfway across the continent, this quilt has remained in the family as a revered heirloom and reminder of President Lincoln's compassion for a young widow.

Young Choctaw mother with baby.
Oklahoma Historical Society photo.

⌄ LOG CABIN

Maker: Hana Brenton Randle (1869-1963). Made in Cooeyescooey District of Cherokee Nation, now Nowata County, Oklahoma, 1886.

Owner: Janifer K. Brown, great-granddaughter.

Pieced: 73" x 68"; cotton: assorted brown, black and other colors; not quilted.

Quiltmaker Hana Randle was born in northern Indian Territory into the Delaware Indian tribe. She married James Tulles Randall when she was fourteen years old and made this Log Cabin quilt when she was expecting her second child at age seventeen. She had a total of eight children.

As a base for the pieced blocks, she used fabric from sacks that had originally contained sugar.

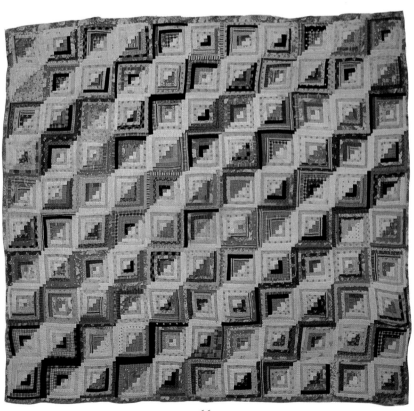

FAMILY HISTORY QUILT

Maker: **Leona Kersey Noe (1878-1957). Made at Coweta, Wagoner County, Oklahoma, 1933-1936.**

Owner: **Ophelia Johnston, daughter.**

Pieced and embroidered: **85" x 76½"; cotton: white blocks with multi-colored threads; hand quilted.**

Before official government records were kept of marriages, births and deaths, families often kept their records in a family Bible. However, this quilt, made over a span of several years, records in handwriting that was then embroidered, the story of a family. Written on the quilt are records of marriages, names of babies born and family deaths. Examination of dates of birth and death indicates that a number of the babies died the day of birth or within a few weeks or months, attesting to the high infant mortality rate of bygone years. The quilt provides a rare glimpse of family life recorded on fabric.

PETER COTTONTAIL AND FRIENDS ➤

Maker: **Daisy Hamilton (1888-1953). Made in Tulsa, Oklahoma, 1937.**

Owner: **Jack W. and JoAnne Dragoun, great-grandson.**

Applique and embroidery: **45" x 32"; cotton: white with pastels; hand quilted.**

Children of the 1930s were very familiar with the adventures of Peter Cottontail. Daisy Hamilton made this precious crib quilt for her granddaughter, Claudette Davis Dragoun, who, in turn, gave it to her son, Jack and his wife JoAnne for their expected child, now arrived. Her name is Kristina Michelle and she was born September 29, 1988, just in time to add her bit of history to this quilt's legacy.

THIS LITTLE PIG WENT TO MARKET

Maker: **Bessie Mable Jackson Shi (1888-1968). Made at Stratford, Garvin County, Oklahoma, 1934-1935.**

Owner: **Mary Josephine Shi Stucker, granddaughter.**

Appliqued and embroidered: **52" x 38"; cotton: pink and white; hand quilted.**

Bessie Shi had two grandchildren born in February, 1933, for whom she made identical quilts based on the "Three Little Pigs" story. Her third grandchild was born in 1934 and received a quilt of the same size but a different pattern. This time the subject was "This Little Pig Went to Market" and it is thought that an area newspaper was the pattern source.

Of Choctaw Indian heritage, Bessie was born in the Jimtown settlement, near Ardmore in Indian Territory, and at age fifteen married Dr. A.H. Shi. In 1907, the railroad came through the area and they moved to Stratford, building the home in which their children and eight grandchildren were born. She was a skilled needlewoman but was also remembered as the first woman in Stratford to learn to drive a car, a feat which many women of her generation never accomplished.

Bessie Jackson Shi (right) and family

DUTCH BONNET GIRL

Maker: Hazel M. Watson Watson (1919-   ). Made at Fitzhugh, Pontotoc County, Oklahoma, early 1930s.

Owner: Hazel Watson Watson

Pieced: 85" x 64"; cotton: pink and white with multi-color crayon art; not quilted.

Hazel Watson was about twelve years old when she made this delightful quilt top during summer vacation from school and she recalls that the purpose of the activity was to give her something creative to do. After carefully tracing Bertha Corbett Babies patterns on fabric, Hazel skillfully colored the figures with crayons and then added her own whimsical backgrounds. The finished product is a charming rendition of the popular pattern.

COLONIAL LADIES

Maker: Ruby Jones Adams (1915-   ). Quilted by maker and her mother, Rella Moon Jones. Made at Gould, Harmon County, Oklahoma, 1929.

Owner: Ruby Adams.

Appliqued and embroidered: 82" x 63"; cotton: multi-colors in figures; hand quilted.

At the time she made the Colonial Ladies quilt, Ruby Jones' parents had moved from the farm to the town of Gould where her father operated a restaurant. Ruby's mother Rella made many pieced quilts, but in 1929, fourteen-year-old Ruby wanted to make the Colonial Ladies. The blocks were pre-stamped and could be earned by selling subscriptions to magazines. Ruby was a good salesperson and earned enough blocks for two quilts. A waitress in her father's cafe, Ruby kept the blocks tucked under the counter and whenever she had a few spare minutes, worked on her quilt.

A LITTLE BOY'S ALPHABET ❯

Maker: Gerald Dixon (1922-   ) Quilted by his mother, Rosa Dixon, and his grandmother, Mary Otis Dixon. Made near Guymon, Texas County, Oklahoma, 1930.

Owner: Gerald Dixon.

Pieced and embroidered: 79½" x 66"; cotton: red and white; hand quilted.

Gerald Dixon's early schooling was at Eula, a one-room country school about fifteen miles northwest of Guymon in the Oklahoma panhandle. In this school, one teacher had 51 students in grades one through eight.

At age eight, Gerald had a sickness that kept him home from school several weeks. To keep him occupied, his mother taught him to embroider and gave him the ABC patterns to make. His mother and grandmother assembled and quilted his efforts and saved the quilt for Gerald until he had a home of his own.

As a quiltmaker, this was his first and last effort, but it did win him a first place award at the Texas County Free Fair when he was eight.

Bud Haws

NINE PATCH ❯

Maker: Hershel H. "Bud" Haws (1921-1974). Made at Welch, Craig County, Oklahoma, 1931-32.

Owner: Phyllis Diane Haws, wife.

Pieced: 84" x 66"; cotton: variety of scraps with blue and white; hand quilted.

Hershel Haws' Nine Patch quilt, made when he was age ten, in a symbolic way parallels his own life, serving as a scrapbook might in evoking memories for his family and heirs. Times were hard on the farm in eastern Oklahoma where Bud grew up. His mother Juanita frequently made quilts from usable portions of discarded clothing, such as shirt tails. Often suffering severe pain in his feet and legs, especially in cold weather, young Hershel made this Nine Patch for warmth, using scraps found in his mother's sewing basket.

The year 1938 found Bud bound for California like many other "Okies" during the Depression. There he found work as a brakeman, gandy-dancer and conductor with the Western Pacific Railroad. In the fifties, he lost one leg, five years later the other. It was around this time that the Nine Patch left Hershel's possession, eventually finding its way to the care of his mother who stored it away.

The quilt was returned to Hershel and his bride Phyllis in 1962, when it was used only once--on their wedding bed. In 1967, then the parents of four children, the Haws returned to Welch, Oklahoma, and purchased a farm. It was during this time that Bud once again took up quiltmaking. Sadly, he passed away in 1974, leaving his family a legacy of five handmade quilts.

AUTUMN LEAVES

Maker: **Myrtle Baker   (1879-1971). Made at Altamont, Kansas, 1932.**

Owner: **Judy McIntosh.**

Applique and pieced: **94" x 88"; cotton: assorted scraps on white with yellow; prairie point edging; hand quilted.**

This talented quilt artist had three children and made seven quilts for each. To avoid any suggestion of favoritism, Mrs. Baker made three identical quilts in each of seven designs. Most were pieced, but she had skill in applique, too, as shown by this Autumn Leaves quilt featuring hundreds of leaves, each one composed of several pieces of fabric. Of the seven quilts they received, her son Jim Reed and his wife Alma liked this one best. It was never used. Alma Reed said of her mother-in-law, "She never sat down empty-handed. She loved rose gardens and enjoyed painting in oils. She did not like housework."

When the current owner acquired the quilt, she asked questions of the Reeds about the quiltmaker, where it was made, and when it was given to them. She recorded this information so that the quilt's history would remain intact even though the artifact was leaving the family.

AIRPLANE   ❯

Maker: **Bessie McBroom Watson (1899-1977). Made at McCalls Chapel, near Allen in Pontotoc County, Oklahoma, 1930-1939.**

Owner: **Hazel and Tom Watson.**

Pieced: **80" x 66"; cotton: blue, yellow and gold; hand quilted.**

In the 1930s, airplanes were popular attractions: stunt fliers performed at fairs and for a fee people could go for a short ride. Prominent Oklahoman Wiley Post made aviation news and the nation grieved when his plane crashed in 1935, killing him and his famous passenger, Will Rogers. The interest in airplanes was manifested in quilts too, for several different airplane patterns were printed about this time.

Bessie Watson made this quilt for her eleven-year-old son, Nathaniel Tom Watson. She made many quilts while pursuing a career in teaching. She taught elementary grades one through four, high school home economics, science and English. She was a high school principal when she retired in 1962.

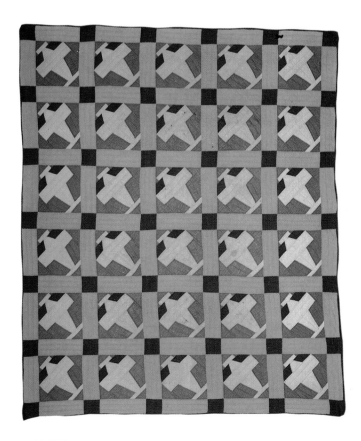

Bessie McBroom Watson

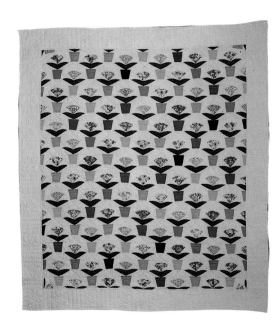

FLOWER IN POT

Maker: **Belle Zona Thompson Jackson (1873-1948). Quilted by Ladies' Auxilliary of St. James Church, Stoney Hill, Missouri, Made in Coal County, Oklahoma, 1936.**

Owner: **Ruth Ann Jackson Fuller, granddaughter.**

Pieced: **82" x 74"; cotton: multi- colored scraps; hand quilted.**

Another mother who made the same pattern for each child was Belle Thompson, wife of Greenwood Jackson, an early day Coal County rancher. They were married at Sacred Heart Church in 1890 and had nine children, seven of whom lived to adulthood. Each was presented with a quilt top. Their daughter, Leatrice Cook Anglin Jackson, kept her top without quilting it and later explained to her daughter, the present owner, that ". . . she was afraid to quilt it as her quilting stitches were not as tiny as Granny Jackson's." In recent years it was sent to a church group in Missouri to be quilted.

It would be hard to imagine a brighter or more cheery pattern than this one and perhaps that is why the maker opted to make seven of them as her way of creating something colorful in the dark days of the Depression years.

SUNBONNET SUE 〉

Maker: **Gladys W. Niemann Weeden (1905-1987). Made near Washington, McClain McClain County, Oklahoma, 1931.**

Owner: **Norma Lea Waugh, daughter.**

Pieced, appliqued and embroidered: **42½" x 34"; cotton: assorted prints with pink set; hand quilted.**

An oft-repeated phrase was, "Idle hands are the devil's workshop" and this adage may have played a part in the extreme popularity of patterns depicting little girl figures busy at a variety of activities. Dozens of different patterns were available in assorted sizes and designs, but the one feature they had in common was that the figure was not idle. This lovely example is based on Eveline Foland's Sunbonnet Sue pattern.

Gladys Weeden made it for her first child, Norma Lea.

Gladys Nieman Weeden

FLOWER BASKET WITH WREATH MEDALLION

Maker: **Marie Magdene Fricke Huelskoetter (1852-1929). Made at Grand Prairie, Illinois, circa 1868.**

Owner: **Hilda Schroder, granddaughter.**

Appliqued: **82" x 75"; cotton: red, green, gold, blue and white solids; ruching on flowers; trapunto grapes; hand quilted.**

    This exuberantly designed quilt was completed by Marie Magdene Fricke when she was sixteen years old. Researchers of Oklahoma's Quilt Heritage Project found a number of these elaborately appliqued quilts made by girls in their teens. Though no two are alike, they are all filled with an originality and extravagance of design that delight the viewer.
    Marie gave her quilt to a granddaughter, Hilda, who brought it to Oklahoma in 1938.

GEOMETRY SAMPLER

Maker: Pawnee High School Geometry Class of 1935. Quilted by Helen Saunders. Made in Pawnee, Pawnee County, Oklahoma, 1935.

Inscribed: Initials of student maker in each block.

Owner: Clella Harris Kelley.

Pieced: 104½ x 71"; cotton: lavender and white; hand quilted.

Miss Kathryn Cunningham had an innovative method of helping her students understand geometry. She selected and bought fabric that was given to each student for designing and sewing blocks of their choice. When complete, the student embroidered his intials on the block and Clella Harris Kelley, current owner of the quilt, helped arrange them and designed a border for the class project. Before her death, Miss Cunningham gave the treasured quilt to its present owner.

DRESDEN PLATE SUNFLOWER >

Maker: Mary Philpott Donar (1898-   ). Made at Ekron, Kentucky, 1936.

Owner: Christine Bicket, granddaughter.

Appliquéd and pieced: 82" x 66"; cotton: scraps with pink and green; hand quilted.

Quilts have sometimes been called "love stitches" and many quilts have been made through the years as gifts for special occasions in loved ones' lives. This bright, beautiful quilt made of period fabrics of the thirties, was made as a high school graduation gift for the current owner when she graduated from Clinton (now Webster) High School in Tulsa, Oklahoma.

Maker: **Dortha Bourbonnais Baxter (1916-   ). Quilted with her mother, Cora Mae Long. Made at Sharon, Woodward County, Oklahoma, 1934.**

Owner: **Donna Baxter-Trice, daughter.**

Pieced: **84" x 66"; cotton: orange and white solids; hand quilted.**

Dortha Bourbonnais hand pieced this quilt at age eighteen just after graduation from Sharon High School, before she went to business college in Wichita, Kansas. The pattern was from the *Kansas City Star* newspaper. A quilt frame was set up in an abandoned house, where they quilted during the summer days and sometimes even into the evenings by the light of a coal oil lamp.

Dortha Baxter

DUTCH DOLL   ❯

Maker: **Pauline Jane Bowen Thomas (1883-1955). Made at Purcell, McClain County, Oklahoma, 1935-1938.**

Owner: **Bobby Ray Thomas, grandson.**

Applique, pieced and embroidered: **82" x 69½; cotton: multi-color prints and solids set with red; hand quilted.**

Parents of eight children, quiltmaker Pauline Thomas and her husband, Ether, came to Oklahoma Territory from Texas in 1900, settling near Purcell.

This charming Dutch Doll quilt was made by Pauline for the wedding of her son Lawson in the 1930s. The pattern is of a type published in *The Daily Oklahoman* and *Kansas City Star* newspapers at that time. The quiltmaker made over one hundred quilts between 1897 and 1945.

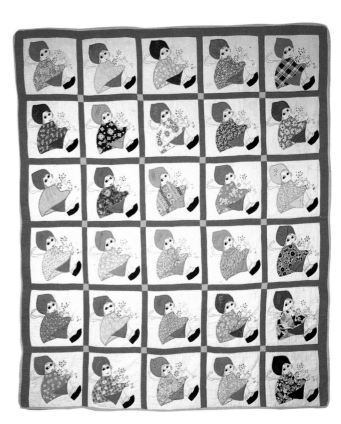

BASKET WITH APPLES (CHERRY BASKET) ❯

Maker: Martha Cordes Kirmse (1879-1967); quilters: the maker and her mother, Margaretha Cordes. Made at Farrar, Missouri, 1900.

Owner: N.K. Rauh, daughter.

Pieced and appliqued: 76" X 72"; cotton: red, green, pink and white solids; hand quilted.

For families living off the land, adversity often forced the children to assume many adult duties. Day to day living was a severe physical challenge, and quilting became a welcome diversion even for the young.

This quiltmaker's father, a farmer of German descent, was disabled by a stroke when his three daughters were very young. The girls helped their mother farm their Missouri land until their respective marriages. Quilting was done only in the winter months–the warmer months were consumed by farm duties.

On her wedding day in 1904, Martha Cordes Kirmse and her husband boarded a train bound for Oklahoma Territory. They settled near Shattuck in Ellis County where their first child, a son, was born in a sod house.

Sod house, c. 1905. Oklahoma Historical Society photo.

76

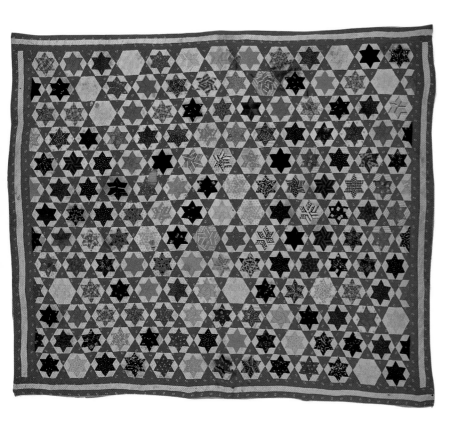

SIX-POINTED STAR

Maker: **Lucinda Hephzibah Chapman (1851-1933). Made near Des Arc, Prairie County, Arkansas, 1912.**

Owner: **Mrs. Betty M. Buchanan, great granddaughter.**

Pieced: **81" x 67"; cotton: maroons and assorted prints; homespun backing; hand quilted.**

Quilts were made for the special events in a person's life and Lucinda Chapman made this one for her granddaughter, Eva Lenora Johnson, when the girl married Walter Andrew Ashby on November 3, 1912. The newlyweds set up housekeeping in Arkansas where Walter farmed and operated a sawmill. He came to Oklahoma as a witness in a court trial and fell in love with the area. After selling most of their Arkansas property, he put their mules, wagon and household belongings on a train car and moved the family to a farm near Bowlegs in Seminole County. The quilt made this and subsequent moves in the area and has now been passed to a descendant of Lucinda's.

SCHOOL HOUSE

Maker: **Minnie McCrea Miller Skaggs (1878-1959). Made at Elmore City, Chickasaw Nation, Indian Territory, circa 1903.**

Owner: **Kathleen Nation, daughter.**

Pieced: **80" x 78"; cotton: aqua and multi-color prints; hand quilted.**

The fabric in this quilt is beautiful and appears to be non-American. The mother of the maker, Frances Nesbitt McCrea, was born in Belfast, Ireland, and later emigrated to Canada to join her husband. He had emigrated earlier and worked to earn money to pay passage for his family. It is very possible that fabric from this generation was saved and used in the 1903 quilt made by the daughter of this couple.

Quiltmaker Minnie McCrea, was born in Canada. When she was about three years of age, her family went by wagon to Arkansas, a journey requiring two months travel since there were no roads or bridges. Minnie married Pat Miller in 1898 in Arkansas. During this period, her husband worked building railroads through Arkansas and eastern Oklahoma and the family was in Garvin County, Oklahoma, when this quilt was made.

TREE OF PARADISE

Maker: **Florence Nonnamaker Griebel (1892-1980). Made near Little River, Rice County, Kansas, 1930-1931.**

Owner: **Pauline Griebel Hamilton, daughter.**

Pieced: **84" x 69"; cotton: green and white; hand quilted.**

Born in Indiana, Florence Nonnamaker taught school in Ohio, Kansas and Oklahoma prior to her marriage to Henry J. Griebel. They settled on the Griebel farm in Rice County, Kansas, near the sod house where her husband had been born. In 1935 the Griebels moved to Lincoln County, Oklahoma. Henry planted the first wheat in a region accustomed to cotton farming; and at harvest time, Florence cooked hearty meals for the hungry crews.

She made many quilts during her lifetime and this one has wonderful workmanship in the piecing. The pattern was from the *Weekly Kansas City Star* and the quilt was rather extravagant for her, for she bought the green and white fabric especially for it, rather than using scraps as she usually did.

GRANDMOTHER'S FAN ❯

Maker: **Nannie Samuel Bruce (1863-1954). Made at Ladonia, Texas, 1885.**

Owner: **Beverly Bruce Creed, granddaughter.**

Pieced and embroidered: **76" x 76"; cotton and velvet: brown, red and white; heat glazed cotton backing; ribbon binding; tied.**

An artist sees things others miss and one wonders if other pioneers in the Denton, Texas, area immediately following the Civil War were aware of the beautiful wild flowers that Nannie Samuel saw. As a young woman she made this very dramatic and distinctive quilt. She drew the wild flowers that she had seen in her surroundings and embroidered each block in a different floral motif using a variety of stitches.

In 1919 the family came to Oklahoma and the quilt went to her son, Fred Bruce, and then later to a granddaughter, the present owner.

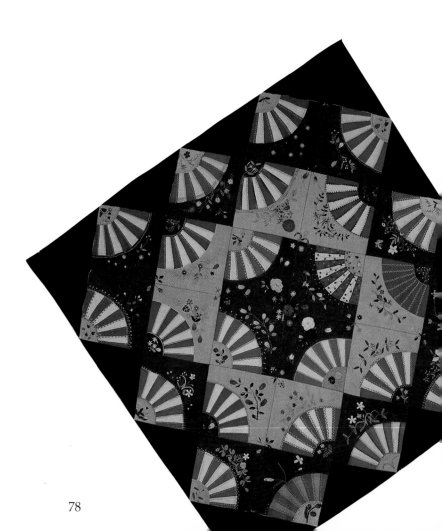

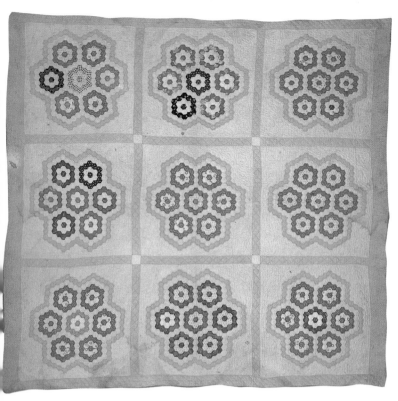

Cora Riley Knight

MOSAIC ⋀

Maker: **Cora Lee Riley Knight (1860-1945). Made at Oxford, Mississippi, circa 1879.**

Owner: **Sherrie Anderson, great granddaughter.**

Pieced: **75" x 70"; cotton: brown prints and solids on white; hand quilted.**

Cora Lee Riley made this quilt in 1879, before her marriage to James Andrew Knight. In 1893 the couple moved to Dublin, Texas, and eight months later on to Tecumseh, Indian Territory. Except for a four year sojourn in Mississippi from 1904-1908, the remainder of the quiltmaker's life was spent at Antioch, Garvin County, Oklahoma. Family records state that Cora Knight bore eleven children and her husband was in the freight hauling business. The family resided on a farm leased from an Indian man with the surname of Pink Bull.

ROCKY ROAD TO KANSAS ⟩

Maker: **Katie B. Long Cummins (1892-1981). Made in Alabama, circa 1900.**

Owner: **Letha King Johnson, cousin.**

Pieced: **78" x 64"; cotton flannel: multi-color prints; home-dyed lining; hand quilted.**

Dark-hued cotton flannel in assorted plaids, stripes and solids was a practical choice for wearing apparel at the turn of the century. Soft and warm, it was used for making shirts, dresses and nightwear so it is logical that remnants found their way into quilts of the era. Yardage of the fabric was frequently purchased to be used as the lining of tied, wool comforters that were the standard bedcover used during cold weather.

The maker of this quilt, Katie Long, was born at Mussel Shoals, Alabama. She married James Leonard Cummins in Alabama and their moves took them first to Welder, Texas. In 1903 they traveled by covered wagon to Pecan Grove in Indian Territory and there rented a farm from a landowner known in the area as Old Man Pugh.

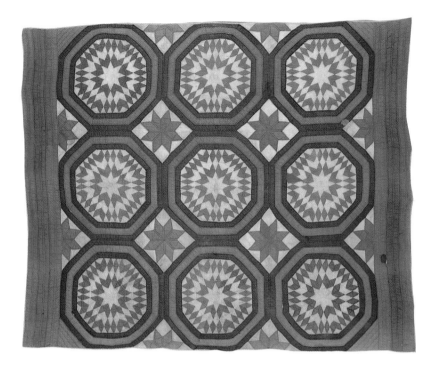

STARBURST WITH STAR SETTING

Maker: **Caroline Criner Eddings (1880-1925). Made at Mt. Judia, Newton County, Arkansas, 1903.**

Owner: **Bethel Eddings Lee, daughter.**

Pieced: **76" x 62"; cotton: tan and blue; hand quilted.**

This quilt of home dyed fabric was made while Caroline Criner was in her twenties, teaching in Arkansas. For six years she was the teacher in a one-room school with students ranging from small children in grade one through teenagers trying to complete the eighth grade work.

In 1912, she and her husband, Frank Eddings, moved by covered wagon to northeast Coal County in Oklahoma, where they reared nine children.

BASKET OF FLOWERS

Maker: **Mary Gowey (1868-1955). Made at Newkirk, Kay County, Oklahoma, circa 1920.**

Owner: **LeBron Zolbe.**

Applique: **90" x 68"; cotton sateen: rose and pink; hand quilted.**

Dr. Herman Gowey attended medical school in Keokuk, Iowa. When he graduated, he came to Oklahoma Territory where he met Mary. She was a traveling nurse, riding horseback from her home to take care of the early settlers. She was fifteen years older than the new, young doctor; but they married and together served the people of the area. Their home was the site of the first territorial hospital in north central Oklahoma. She was an accomplished rider and appreciated fine horses, preferring five-gaited thoroughbreds and Tennessee Walkers.

Mary Gowey

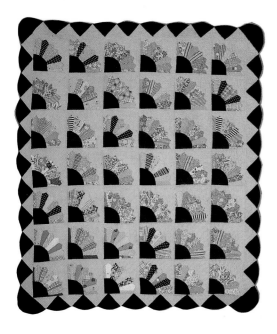

GRANDMOTHER'S FAN

Maker: Cora Curry Millspaugh (1892-1952). Made at Clinton, Custer County, Oklahoma, 1934.

Owner: Mr. and Mrs. John Millspaugh.

Appliqued and pieced: 78" x 66"; cotton: yellow and black with prints; hand quilted.

It was in addition to her myriad duties as a farm wife that Mrs. Millspaugh pursued her interest in quilting. For her Grandmother's Fan quilt, one of twelve she created, the quiltmaker used scraps from her sewing, but chose a black solid and bright yellow to set off the prints. A stunning lattice effect was the result.

FARM FRIENDLINESS

Maker: Origin unknown. Made 1930s.

Owner: Yvonne Bender.

Pieced: 82" x 67"; cotton: scrap with red, white and blue; hand quilted.

The current owner's father was an attorney, practicing law at Thomas in Custer County, Oklahoma. It is very possible that this quilt may have been payment for a legal debt but its origin will remain a mystery.

HOUSE

Maker: Ruth Naomi Hendricks (1907-1981). Made near Mangum, Green County, Oklahoma, 1931.

Owner: Joy Hendricks, sister-in-law.

Pieced: 79" x 78"; cotton: red, white and green; hand quilted.

Creating and caring for the home was central in most women's lives. It is not surprising then that the House pattern has been a popular one with quiltmakers and this quilt made by Ruth Hendricks using the complementary colors of red and green is a lovely example.

DOUBLE T ∧

Pieced: 85½" x 78"; cotton: black with scrap;
hand quilted.

SUNFLOWER ∧

Pieced: 88" x 79"; cotton: brown and green;
hand quilted.

COLLECTION MADE BY ANDREWS SISTERS

Makers: **Martha (1862-1949), Margarette (1868-1936), Rachel (1871-1962) Andrews. Made near Rocky, Washita County, Indian Territory, circa 1900.**

Owner: **Dortha M. Cannon Bass, granddaughter of Elijah Cannon, quiltmakers' uncle.**

Sisters Martha, Margarette and Rachel Andrews were from a family of twelve children. Their parents, Ezekiel and Sarah Cannon Andrews, migrated westward, their children's birthplaces were found on record in Alabama, Arkansas and Oklahoma. About 1901, the three maiden sisters came by covered wagon to live near their uncle, Elijah Wiley Barbee Cannon, who had homesteaded near Rocky in Oklahoma Territory. Martha, the eldest of the three, filed on the eighty acres and for the next thirty-two years, the women farmed their land with a team of horses. They had promised their mother on her deathbed that they would never marry, and they were true to their word. Their lives consisted of their farm work and quilting. They made quilts, many of them, and almost always there were three from each pattern.

General characteristics of their collection indicate that the sisters preferred pieced, traditional patterns of predominately dark hues with either a deep green or red appearing in most of the quilts. Some have vegetable dyed backing and all have thick batts.

Andrews Family

82

DUCK PADDLE ⌃

Pieced: 84" x 65"; cotton: scraps set with blue; hand quilted.

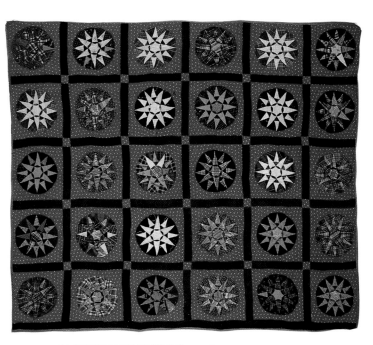

ROLLING PINWHEEL ⌃

Pieced: 87" x 75"; cotton: multi colors with red and black; hand quilted.

DOUBLE Z ❯

Pieced: 84" x 78½" cotton: scraps set with green; hand quilted.

83

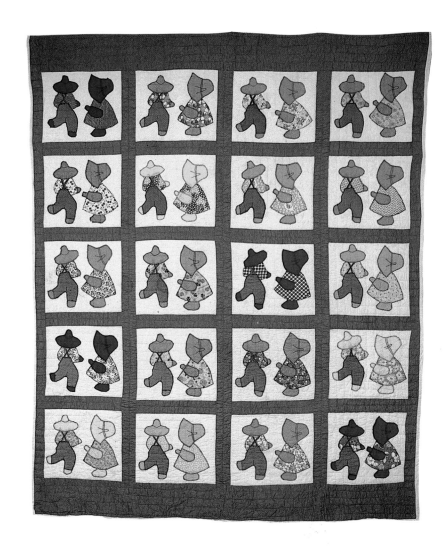

DUTCH GIRL AND BOY

Maker: **Mary Alice "Mollie" Walker Baker (1886-1964). Made at Mountain Park, Kiowa County, Oklahoma, circa 1937.**

Owner: **Mrs. Edward Graham, niece.**

Applique, pieced and embroidered: **82" x 68"; cotton: multi-color with green sashing; hand quilted.**

Mollie's life started near Milsap, Texas. She moved to a farm in the Chickasaw Nation near Ardmore with her parents in 1892, and in 1899 became the bride of Robert T. Baker at the nearby community of Purdy. He was a Baptist preacher and served a large number of small congregations with the family moving from place to place every few years.

The mother of nine children born between 1901 and 1923, Mollie made this quilt in 1930 when her youngest had just started to school. She enjoyed doing things for others and this whimsical, cheerful quilt with the boy figure in motion, was made for her niece, the current owner.

Mary Walker Baker

› MORNING GLORY

Maker: Rohesa Anne Harmon Elrod (1867-1949). Made at Lovell, Logan County, Oklahoma, circa 1930.

Owner: Ruby Wehrenberg.

Applique: 74½" x 68"; cotton: blue on ecru; hand quilted.

This Morning Glory quilt with its ties to the floral applique tradition of the twenties and thirties, is one of a pair made by Rohesa Elrod. This well-balanced and meticulously executed quilt was probably made from a published pattern.

The quiltmaker came to Oklahoma Territory from Indiana in 1900. The mother of seven, she made many quilts for her children and grandchildren and in her diary made reference to "going to quilting bees."

BASKET OF DAISIES ⌄

Maker: Nettie Wiedenkofer Holt (1865-1939). Completed by daughter Emma Pratt (1893-   ). Made near Arnett, Ellis County, Oklahoma, circa 1930.

Owner: Emma Pratt, daughter.

Applique: 94" x 80"; cotton: white with green, black and prints; hand quilted.

Born in Mississippi, Nettie's young adult years were spent in Missouri. In 1900 she came with her family to Oklahoma Territory, traveling six weeks in a covered wagon. They filed on land west of Arnett in far western Oklahoma and lived in a dugout for eight years.

Fabric originally manufactured to be used in feed sacks was recycled by talented Nettie Holt to become the lovely daisies in this quilt. She was a very good seamstress and sewed for her family of thirteen children, plus making garments for neighbors. Before her death in 1939, she made a special quilt for each of her eleven living children.

Nettie Wiedenkofer Holt

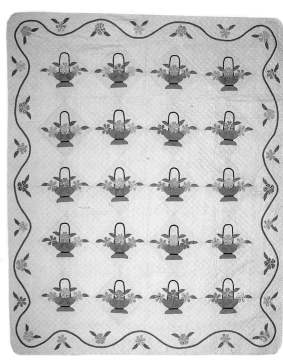

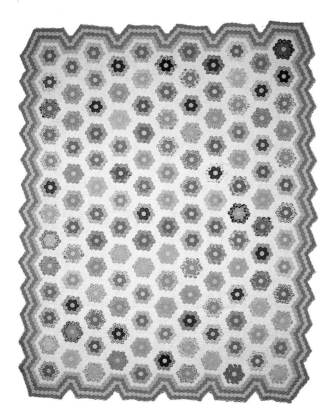

◄ GRANDMOTHER'S FLOWER GARDEN

Maker: Ella Ebernissee Schroder (1864-1959). Made in Oklahoma City, Oklahoma, circa 1930s.

Pieced: 87" x 71"; cotton: multi prints and solids; hand pieced.

Ella Bernissee Shroder

Patterns with hexagon-shaped pieces were found in 19th century "Mosaic" quilts, but they reached their peak of popularity in the second quarter of the twentieth century with a pattern called Grandmother's Flower Garden. Untold thousands of quiltmakers made quilts of this design. Judging by the large number of Flower Garden quilts found across the nation by documentation surveys, family members still treasure these mementos of their mothers and grandmothers.

A lovely example of this favored pattern with a four row border is this quilt made by Ella Schroder. Born in Sheboygan, Wisconsin, into a family of thirteen children, she knew all about hard work. At age thirteen she was "loaned" to other families to help with housework. Married in Iowa, she moved to Missouri and then to Oklahoma where her husband in 1902 bought a relinquishment on a Caddo County farm. In her late years, she pieced and quilted Double Wedding Ring and Grandmother's Flower Garden quilts for a $25.00 fee to supplement her limited income.

FLOWER GARDEN BASKET   ►

Maker: Luticia Reeves Fancher King (1869-1934). Made near Breckenridge, Garfield County, Oklahoma, circa 1931.

Owner: Mary Hermanski Briggs, granddaughter.

Pieced: 90" x 82"; cotton: solids with green hexagon setting; hand quilted.

Like so many others, Luticia King made quilts over a long span of time. In her later years, she made quilts for all of the grandchildren and great-grandchildren as part of their legacy from this woman whose life in Oklahoma started with homesteading.

Her husband made the Run alone into the Cherokee Strip Outlet in 1893. A wooden frame house with four rooms was built; and then Luticia, with two small children and a hired cowboy, made the journey in a covered wagon from Henryetta, Texas, to their new home twelve miles northeast of Enid, Oklahoma Territory.

Luticia Fancher King

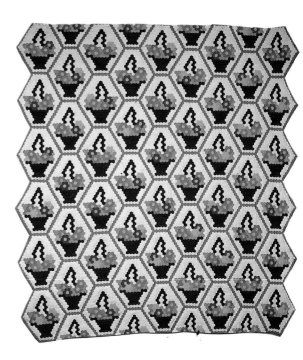

‹ NEW YORK BEAUTY

Maker: Martha Susan Wooley Pettyjohn (1844-1914). Made near Harrison, Arkansas, 1902.

Owner: Drexel Wint Malone.

Pieced: 82" x 68"; cotton: tan, yellow and red; hand quilted.

Quilts were made for all the milestones of life-births, graduation, weddings, and even death. In some early day communities, it was customary to use a quilt to line the homemade wooden casket. This quilt was made for that purpose by the grandmother of Walter Darris Eoff.

At age six, Darris broke his arm. The bone protruded, infection set in and the arm was amputated in two surgeries, first at the elbow and then, when the infection continued to spread, at the shoulder. Surgery took place on the family's kitchen table and it was assumed that he would not live. His grandmother, Mrs. Pettyjohn, made this quilt to be buried with him. He recovered, moved with his family to Indian Territory and then later to western Oklahoma. Darris Eoff died in Shawnee, Oklahoma, in 1954 at the age of sixty years. Of course by then customs had changed, and his "death quilt" survives as a special heirloom.

UNKNOWN DESIGN ›

Maker: Rachel Randolph Stanley (1835-1919). Made at Madras, Red River County, Texas, 1896.

Owner: Kate Wauhop Phillips, great-granddaughter.

Pieced: 81" x 68"; cotton: red, green and gold; hand quilted.

Mental health specialists have long recognized that working with colorful fabric or thread as a medium, creating from it an item of useful beauty, is therapeutic. History records that quiltmaking was commonly done in military hospitals as rehabilitation for those who suffered shell shock and severe depression following the Civil War and WWI. Perceptive, caring family members have understood the value of this special therapy also.

Kate Phillips, the current owner of this quilt writes: "Rachel Randolph Stanley was born in Kentucky and later lived in Texas. When her husband Gilbert died, she lived with her daughter and son-in-law, Settie and Charlie Chapman. He was a farmer and money was scarce. One morning as Charlie left the house for the fields he noticed that his mother-in-law was 'low in spirit.' He came in from his work about noon, hitched the team to the wagon and drove seven miles to Clarksville, Texas, where he bought the fabric for this quilt. When he gave it to her she immediately brightened up and got right into piecing this quilt."

The design appears to be the maker's own creation although it contains elements of known patterns. The cotton for the batting was grown on the farm and hand carded for this quilt.

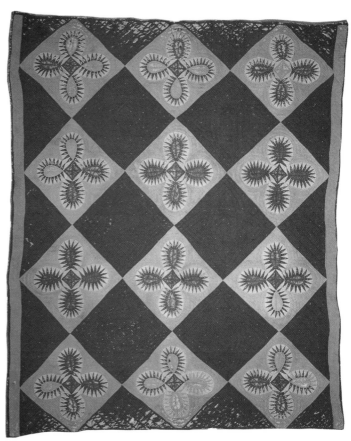

GOOSE IN THE POND

Maker: **Millie Pickens Pratt McLish (c.1839-1929). Made at Bethel, near Lebanon in Chickasaw Nation, Indian Territory, 1907.**

Owner: **Hattie Pratt, granddaughter-in-law.**

Pieced: **82½" x 67"; cotton: scrap; hand quilted.**

Oklahoma was settled by a great diversity of peoples, all of whom brought customs and traditions with them. Burial customs are among those most closely held and are apt to be continued in a new land. Among the Chickasaw people, a quilt was made for a child, then saved till his death when it was used to keep the body "warm" until it could be buried. In some areas, the quilt was then placed on top of the wooden casket as it was lowered into the ground, thus keeping the dirt from making so much noise as the grave was filled. It was a way of expressing compassion and caring for family members.

This quilt was made in 1907 by Millie McLish, a full-blood Chickasaw, for her grandson, Henry Pratt. She made the top from scraps of family clothing, carded her own cotton batt, and quilted it on frames that hung from the ceiling of her home.

LONE STAR >

Maker: **Margret Brown Davis (1873-1965). Made in Jack County, Texas, 1909.**

Owner: **Mildred Davis Forsythe, daughter.**

Pieced and appliqued: **92" x 85"; cotton: variety of prints plus red and white; hand quilted.**

Margret Davis pieced this Lone Star quilt from dresses of her daughter Letha who passed away in 1908 at the age of eighteen. This was done as a tribute to her daughter and as a remembrance.

Sadly, Mrs. Davis pieced another quilt for the same reason only three years later in 1911–this time a Mosaic Diamond Field for a daughter only thirteen years of age at her death.

Chapter V

NEIGHBORHOODS

Extended family, neighbors, church and social groups were very important to the families of early Oklahoma. Isolated, pioneer living with no easy means of communication made women grateful for opportunities to get together. Idle visiting was unacceptable but it was all right to work together at a quilting frame and catch up on the neighborhood news at the same time. In addition to turning out practical, needed household items, there was much sharing of advice on a wide variety of topics. Making quilts to be used as fundraisers for community projects was common during the years when women had little opportunity to earn money on their own.

The Oil Fields of Oklahoma

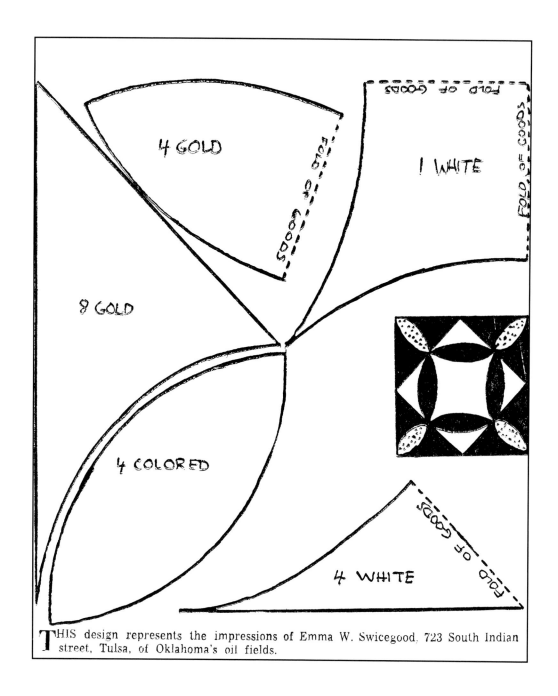

4 GOLD

FOLD OF GOODS

FOLD OF GOODS

1 WHITE

FOLD OF GOODS

9 GOLD

4 COLORED

FOLD OF GOODS

4 WHITE

THIS design represents the impressions of Emma W. Swicegood. 723 South Indian
street, Tulsa, of Oklahoma's oil fields.

FLOWER GARDEN WITH PICKET FENCE

Maker: Pernety Arno Billings Faulkner (1892-1978). Made near Gotebo, Kiowa County, Oklahoma, circa 1935.

Owner: Bettie Faulkner Buchanan, daughter.

Pieced, crayon colored, embroidered: **90" x 80"; cotton: varied with blue and white; hand quilted.**

Neighborliness and sharing were trademarks of communities in Oklahoma during the Depression years. Pernety Faulkner found the patterns for this quilt in the *Daily Oklahoman* starting in the fall of 1929. Needing fabric for the project, she agreed to trade some quilting time to Mrs. Arthur Woods, proprietor of Cooperton General Store, in exchange for the needed yardage. She used ordinary crayons to color and shade the various flowers, then pressed the fabric on the wrong side to set the colors. Silk embroidery thread outlines the flowers and stems.

Pernety Billings Faulkner

FLOWER FRIENDSHIP ➤

Maker: Emma Holt Pratt (1893-   ) and members of the Four-Mile Quilt Club. Made at Arnett, Ellis County, Oklahoma, 1935.

Owner: Emma Pratt.

Pieced, appliqued and embroidered: **94" x 80"; cotton: pink, blue, red, pink and yellow on white; hand quilted.**

Many groups made friendship quilts, for social relationships were deeply intertwined with the basic need to provide warmth for the family. One such group was the Four-Mile Quilt Club of which Emma Pratt, now age 95, was a member. Club members were rural neighbors living within a radius of four miles of the Tierce Chapel Church building located six miles west of Arnett. These ladies met twice a month in homes of members over a period of twenty years from 1932 to 1952.

In 1936, every member made one block for a friendship quilt. Emma Pratt created blue stars in pink sashes to frame the blocks and added white borders. The hand quilting on this marvelous quilt is exquisite attesting to the skills of the members of the Four-Mile Quilt Club.

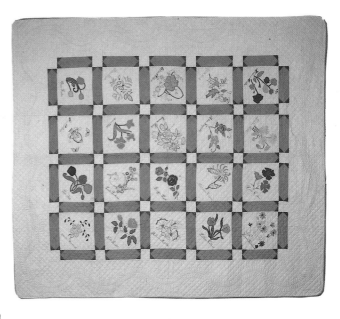

PETUNIA FRIENDSHIP QUILT ➤

Maker: Ona Waggoner Cross (1890-1983). Made at Wewoka, Seminole County, Oklahoma, 1938.

Owner: Iona C. Guilford, daughter.

Pieced and appliqued: 86" x 76"; cotton: tints of lavender plus green; hand quilted.

Two events of historical significance in Oklahoma had impact on the life of Ona Waggoner Cross: the 1889 Land Run and the discovery of vast oil and gas deposits in the state. The nation's first land run brought Charles and Adelaide Waggoner from Kansas to what is now Logan County, Oklahoma. Their homestead, still in the family's possession, was the site of the dugout where daughter Ona was born.

Ona married in 1911, and by 1931 the Cross family was living in Wewoka in the Greater Seminole area, site of an oil field which led the nation in petroleum production from 1925 through 1929. Their home was in an oil camp in a hastily constructed frame house. It was then that Ona joined the Petunia Flower Garden Club, an organization of wives from oil company camps owned by Sinclair, Gulf, Prairie, ITIO and Magnolia. Meeting monthly with the goal of beautifying the camps, the women formed close friendships. Through the exchange of quilt blocks, these precious memories were preserved.

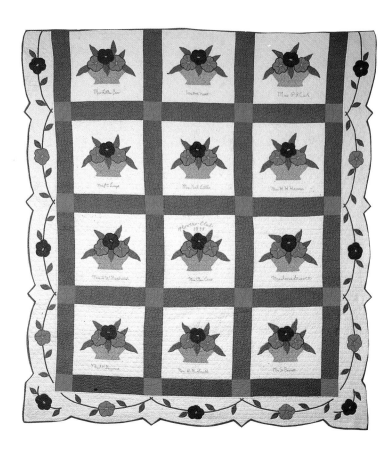

FRIENDSHIP ALBUM ➤

Makers: Lucy Pierce (1880-1946) and Iva Pierce (1902-1986). Made at Eagle City, Blaine County, Oklahoma, 1922-1923.

Owner: Effie Pierce, daughter-in-law of Lucy Pierce.

Pieced: 92" x 68"; cotton: variety of scraps plus blues; hand quilted.

Lucy Pierce and daughter Iva regularly worked together and made many quilts through the years. For this keepsake quilt, relatives, friends and neighbors made blocks, signed and embroidered their names, and presented them to Iva. Born in the family's half-dugout farm home, Iva spent her lifetime assisting area families at times of childbirth and sickness and these blocks were a special gesture of their friendship and love for her. The traditional, overall fan design was used for the quilting stitches.

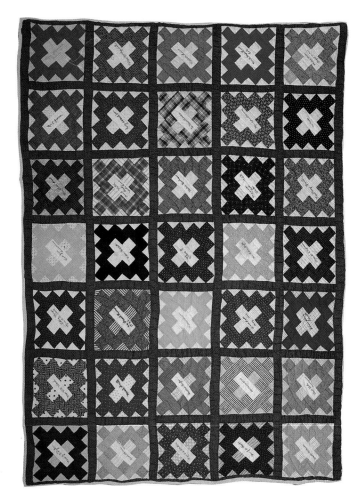

Lucy Pierce

92

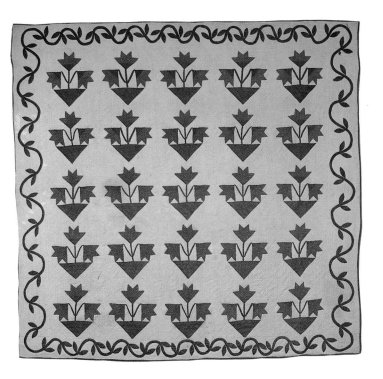

LOG CABIN, COURT HOUSE STEPS ❯

Maker: Jane Phillips (1882-1978). Quilted by Lawton Baptist Church quilting group. Made at Lawton, Comanche County, Oklahoma, 1920s.

Owner: Hope Wickliffe.

Pieced: 80" x 74"; cotton: blue, maroon, multi-color prints; hand quilted.

This Court House Steps setting of the Log Cabin pattern was pieced by Jane Phillips, but quilted by a church group, still a common practice today.

FRIENDSHIP ❯

Maker: Families of World War I Servicemen. Made at Stillwater, Payne County, Oklahoma. Top made in 1917, completed in 1929.

Owner: Sheerar Museum, Stillwater, Oklahoma.

Pieced, appliqued and embroidered: 84" x 84"; wool: black, army green uniforms, red; tied.

Completed in 1929, this quilt was a fund-raiser for American Legion Auxilary Post 129 to build the American Legion building in Stillwater, Oklahoma. Each individual whose name appears on the quilt paid 25¢ to have his name included. There are 520 names; Gold Star Mothers are grouped toward the center, names of some who served in World War I are included, and there is also one three digit telephone number.

The quilt was raffled and the winner donated the quilt back to the Legion Post after the building was completed. It remained in the post until 1974, at which time the quilt was donated to the Sheerar Museum.

❮ NORTH CAROLINA LILY

Maker: Origin unknown. circa 1850.

Owner: Rena Penn Brittan.

Pieced and appliqued: 83" x 78"; cotton: red, green and white; hand quilted.

Wider than it is long, this lovely quilt with its double rows of fine quilting stitches had a long, unrecorded history when it came to the present owner's family. Where it was made and how it got to Oklahoma is not known. During World War I it was raffled in Waukomis, Garfield County, Oklahoma, to raise funds for war bonds. No doubt someone donated it to be used as the prize in the raffle, and it was won by the R.N. Brittan family. Tradition says that all the residents of this small town had bought chances in this patriotic endeavor. It was held in high regard by the lucky family that won it, and was never used, but carefully stored in a cedar chest through the years.

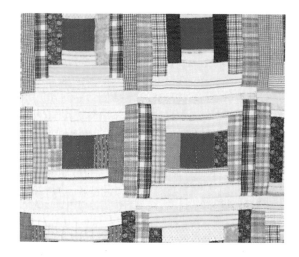

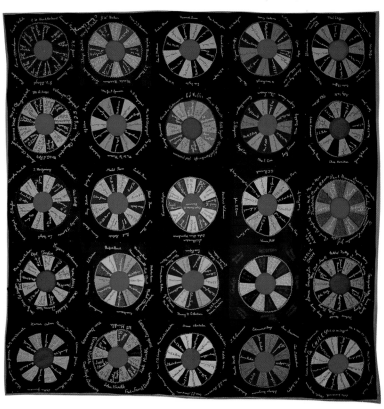

Pearl Judy Maple

CATTLE BRAND DESIGN

Maker: **Pearl Judy Maple (1883-1959). Made at the Maple YL Ranch, Beaver County, Oklahoma, 1939.**

Owner: **Mark M. Mayo, grandson.**

Appliqued, pieced and embroidered: **84" x 75"; cotton: red, yellow, black and tan on white; hand quilted.**

This quilt records early ranch history of far northwest Oklahoma. Cattle brands of the various ranches are depicted in embroidery along with the dates the owners were active in the cattle business. Embroidery of wildlife indigenous to the region is also included along the bottom of this quilt made by rancher Judy Maple, who continued daily horseback rides up into her 80's.

F. B. Severs Ranch House. Oklahoma Historical Society photo.

FRIENDSHIP QUILTS

A basic pattern is frequently modified as quilters add their own interpretation to it. The quilt below and those on the following page have several things in common– each was made as a birthday remembrance, all were made in western Oklahoma within a ten year time span, each is a friendship quilt with quilt blocks made by various individuals. In addition, all three are a variation of a design called Gothic Windows but examination of the quilts provides an interesting study in adaptations and invites speculation as to the reasons for the changes.

FRIENDSHIP

Maker: **Allie May Wallace Hostetter (1879-1975). Made at Foss, Washita County, Oklahoma, 1925.**

Owner: **C.L. Hostetter, son.**

Pieced and appliqued: **79" x 87"; cotton; hand quilted.**

This quilt was made in honor of Allie May Hostetter's forty-sixth birthday and this seems quite appropriate since quilts had always had a place in her background and life. Her mother, Lavina Gates Chapman, left Wisconsin with her parents in the year of 1859 to move to Kansas. Mrs. Chapman cites in her journal after an encounter with raiding Indians, "I cooked breakfast for fifty-two the next morning. That night spread quilts on the floor, all that could get on a quilt was bedded, while the men went watching for the incoming savages."

Allie May was born in Kansas, married in 1897 and moved to western Oklahoma Territory in 1902, homesteading on a farm. She was a charter member of the Homemakers Home Demonstration Club at Foss which was organized in 1929 with nine members.

FRIENDSHIP

Maker: Virgil Payne Wogmon (1893-1968). Made near Elk City, Beckham County, Oklahoma, 1931.

Owner: Mildred L. Wogmon and Elizabeth Wogmon Baber, daughters.

Pieced and appliqued: 88" x 88"; cotton; hand quilted.

On the Sunday nearest the birthday of the different ladies in the Bales community north of Elk City, a dinner was held at that person's home and quilt blocks given to the honoree. She would assemble the blocks, put the top in a quilting frame, and as neighbors had time, they would come and help quilt. The Bales community in which the Wogmon family lived centered around a two-room country school building that was also used for other neighborhood activities.

FRIENDSHIP ➤

Maker: Lizzie Burch Palmer Johnston (1885-1966). Made near Putnam, Dewey County, Oklahoma, 1937.

Owner: Bertha Palmer Haggard, daughter.

Pieced and appliqued: 80" x 60" cotton: hand quilted.

The quiltmaker's daughter cut out the blocks and they were given to friends and neighbors to be embroidered. The finished blocks were returned to Lizzie on her fifty-seventh birthday, she set them together and did the quilting.

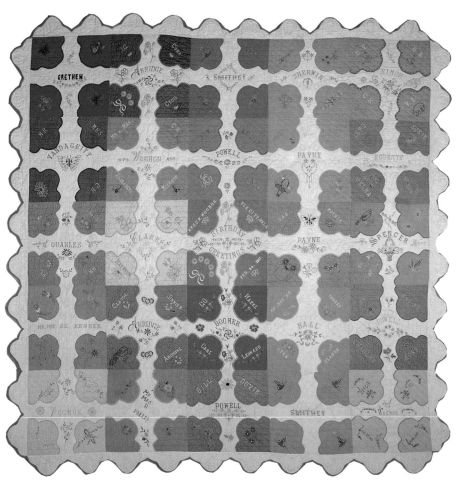

‹ ### RAINBOW (Trip Around the World)

Maker: Ellen Arney Roberts (1894-1978). Made at Buffalo, Harper County, Oklahoma, circa 1935.

Owners: Corinne Roberts Beck and Orma Lee Cotter, daughters.

Pieced: 91" x 76"; cotton: rainbow solids; hand quilted.

Finding exactly the right shades of a desired color has always been a challenge for quiltmakers. In the 1930s, Ellen Roberts and several friends exchanged fabrics with one another and finally had to dye some to obtain the colors needed for Rainbow quilts. The goal was to make a quilt using solid colors of the rainbow with five shades of each hue. Each person in the group set their quilt together differently. Mrs. Roberts set two inch squares (1½" inches finished) on point to achieve a diamond effect with her 3,233 pieces of fabric.

The quilt was never used and stored away except for special occasions when it was shown to guests and family members. Following her death, her widower gave it to the present owners.

DESERT ROSE **›**

Maker: Sarah Glezen Kelso (1864-d. date unknown). Made in Indiana, circa 1935.

Owner: Marcia Boyington Carroll.

Pieced and appliqued: 87" x 80"; cotton: green, yellow and white, plus a variety of scraps; embroidery on flowers; hand quilted.

This Desert Rose quilt combines several popular design elements of the 1930s–stars, diamonds (forming hexagons) and flowers. Sarah Kelso's polished skills included faultless applique, meticulous piecing and fine hand quilting. She left this quilt to her daughter and namesake, Sarah Hopkins.

In bygone years, people frequently lived in the same place for decades and neighbors not only depended upon each other but became the closest of friends. An example of this was the quiltmaker's daughter Sara Hopkins, and the mother of the current owner, Mrs. Boyington. They lived just across the street from each other and enjoyed many of the same activities. They spent many afternoons admiring each other's treasured quilts.

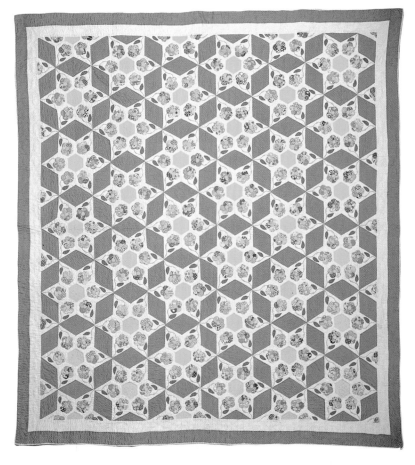

‹ **FRIENDSHIP SAMPLER**

Makers: **Lola White Byram (1896-1974) and Ladies of the First Baptist Church. Made in Granite, Greer County, Oklahoma, 1932.**

Owner: **Shirley F. Pfrehm, daughter.**

Pieced: **76" x 66"; cotton and silk: variety of scraps plus lavendar; hand quilted.**

Lola Byram's daughter Shirley writes, "Ladies of the First Baptist Church in Granite made the quilt for a money-making project. Each lady making a block was to donate one penny for each piece in her block and the one with the most pieces was to win the quilt. My mother asked father if they could afford over $5.00 if she could get over 500 pieces in her block. Dad said they would rake it up someway for the church. My mother won the quilt with the 616 pieces she put in her twelve-inch block."

SCROLL ›

Maker: **Tabitha Ann Taylor Shaffer (1856-1937). Quilted by maker and Natola Maree Shaffer Lamar (1893-) Made at Coyle, Logan County, Oklahoma, 1930.**

Owner: **Maree Shaffer Lamar.**

Appliqued: **84" x 82"; cotton: rose and white; hand quilted.**

The Shaffers came from Iowa in January of 1900 and bought a school lease in Payne County, east of Coyle, Oklahoma. They farmed until 1927 when they moved into town. Through the years, Mrs. Shaffer and her daughter, Natola Maree made many quilts together before and after her marriage. At age ninety-five, Maree Shaffer Lamar continues to quilt several hours each day and even threads her own needles.

Though published patterns were plentiful and available from many sources during the 1930s, Tabitha Shaffer created her own original, dramatic design for this visual delight she calls Scroll.

Maggie Clark Foulk

NOSEGAY ❯

Maker: **Maggie Clark Foulk (1859-1945). Made at Camargo, Dewey County, Oklahoma, 1936.**

Owner: **Mrs. Alex B. Robinson.**

Pieced: **92" x 80"; cotton: variety of scrap prints plus green, pink and white; hand quilted.**

This 1936 Nosegay quilt is kept by owner Anna Robinson as a cherished remembrance of quiltmaker Maggie Foulk. Mrs. Foulk took Anna, then sixteen and orphaned, into her home in the late 1920s. Though but a modest half-dugout with dirt floor, the home was a haven of love to Anna as she returned each day from her work "pulling cotton." Anna and her "Aunt Maggie," in a spring-seat buggy, drove to evening church services "with the coyotes howling and the moon shining so beautifully above the trees and canyons."

Maggie Foulk had no children of her own, and so presented this quilt to Anna, the girl she lovingly fostered in her home.

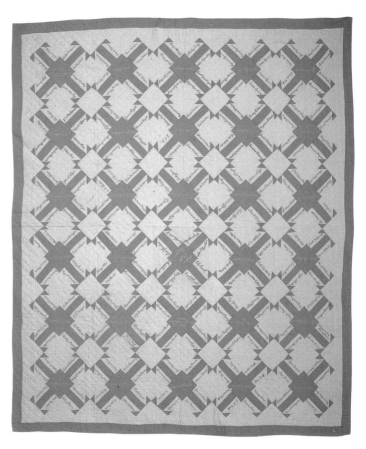

T-SQUARE ❯

Makers: **Ladies of the First Methodist Church. Made at Geary, Blaine County, Oklahoma, 1931.**

Pieced and embroidered: **86" x 76"; cotton: pink and white; hand quilted.**

Made as a fund-raiser, this Mountain Mist pattern quilt also serves as a community history. Although no one remembers exactly what the money was used for, cash was such a precious commodity at the time, it was no doubt spent sparingly and wisely.

The center pink square in each block sold for more money, so most of these contain the name of a business firm in the town and the eight names on white surrounding it are persons who were employees. The usual fee was 25¢ for the center and 10¢ for the other spaces. In some cases, a family took the entire block, with the head of the family having his name in the center and other family names filling the eight spaces. All names were written by a local school teacher, Genevieve Seger, who had lovely penmanship; and then they were embroidered by others in the church who had skills in needlework. It was quilted by women of the church and then sold.

DIAMOND FIELD

Maker: **Florence Shinn Bryant (1887-1956). made at Edmond, Oklahoma County, Oklahoma, 1928-1929.**

Owner: **Vera Bryant Hicks, granddaughter.**

Pieced: **81" x 78"; cotton: pastels with yellow; hand quilted.**

Florence Bryant achieved a delightful new look with her artistic setting of diamond field blocks. The quiltmaker's masterful use of color keeps the viewer's eye moving over the quilt--first seeing a large hexagon, then a star, baby blocks or diamonds. She made many, many quilts according to her granddaughter, and while it is not known if she had a favorite pattern or color, several quilts were "set together" with yellow fabric. Her granddaughter remembers playing under the quilting frame while Mrs. Bryant and her friends quilted.

Florence Shinn Bryant

EAGLE

Maker: Origin unknown. Circa 1910-1920.

Appliqued and embroidered: 76" x 70"; cotton: printed gingham on white; hand quilted.

    Amber A. Henke won this quilt in a raffle sponsored by a church women's group in Billings, Noble County, Oklahoma, about 1930. The printed gingham fabric dates to previous decades and one can only speculate about who may have made this quilt with its unusual design.

LOG CABIN, BARN RAISING SETTING

Maker: **Mary Christine Ray Waggoner (1851-1927). Made in Wabash, Indiana, circa 1900.**

Owner: **Mrs. Betty Parker, granddaughter.**

Pieced: 80" x 70"; cotton: assorted prints, predominantly red, blue, yellow and white; hand quilted.

    The quiltmaker, Mary Waggoner, was a proficient quilter and completed tops for each of her grandchildren. The Log Cabin quilt top had been assembled with its 4,420 pieces, but before it could be quilted, Mary suffered a stroke at her home in Indiana. She needed to be with family so plans were made for her to come to Oklahoma City and stay with her daughter. The only suitable transportation was by train; but as she was unable to sit up, her cot was placed in a box car. Mary traveled this way from Indiana to St. Louis where she transferred to a train with sleeping berths for the remainder of her long journey.

DEATH QUILT ➤

Maker: Alta Alma Gass Curtis (1898-1987), with assistance of family and friends. Made at Hammon, Roger Mills County, Oklahoma, 1924.

Owner: Lahoma Haddock Goldsmith, niece.

Pieced and embroidered: 88" x 70"; wool: garments; not quilted.

At times of tragedy, family and friends express their condolences in many ways. Alta Curtis made this quilt while visiting her sister whose husband had been killed in a hunting accident. She used pieces of his clothing for this wool quilt, embroidered the blocks' borders, and put special stitches in the center portion as a memorial, since it was cut from the garment he was wearing when shot. Others came to assist with the project and the quilt was presented to the widow. She in turn gave it to her daughter, the current owner, and it continued to be tangible evidence of the sympathy and love expressed by family and friends.

STAR WITH TULIPS ➤

Makers: Friends and family of Elizabeth Nolting Volk. Made near Cedar Creek, Nebraska, circa 1870.

Owner: Mrs. Larry Levings, great-granddaughter.

Pieced and appliqued: 78½" x 73"; cotton: gold, brown, green, pink and white; hand quilted.

The family Bible records in German that this quilt was made near Cedar Creek, Nebraska, as a wedding gift for the owner's paternal great-grandmother, Elizabeth Nolting Volk. According to family history, the Star with Tulips was quilted at a quilting bee by friends and family of that rural area. Evidence of the quilt's intended use as a wedding gift is revealed by numerous hearts quilted over the surface. Choice of colors and typical tulip floral motifs reveal the strong German Lutheran influence.

Elizabeth brought her wedding quilt to Oklahoma Territory in 1903 when her family moved to a farm near Renfrow in Grant County.

Chapter VI

CURRENT EVENTS

Long before women were allowed to vote, they expressed their political opinions by making quilts with names like "Whig Rose" which may or may not have been their husband's chosen party. Economic changes, new inventions, current events in the state, nation and world affected the family and frequently a new quilt pattern was created in response. Quilts in this section were made as an expression of affirmation, or as a means of coping with difficulties brought on by events like economic depression, drought and war.

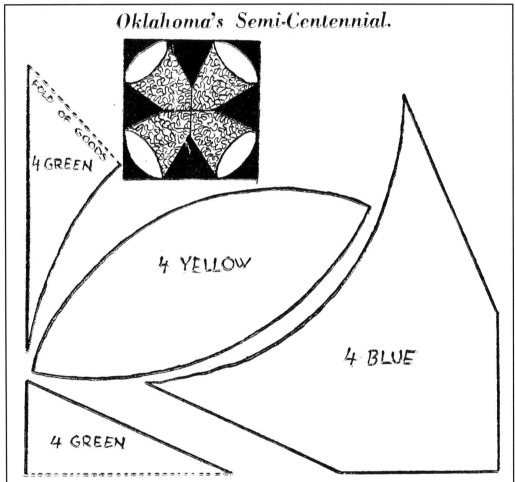

THIS IS a tribute to the Sooner state which this year is celebrating the semi-centennial anniversary of its statehood. The design comes from Emma W. Swicegood, 723 South Indian street, Tulsa.

WHIG ROSE WITH CURRANTS

Maker: Margaret McClure. Made in Virginia, circa 1850.

Owners: Irene Wilson and Sallie Jo Carder, great-nieces.

Appliqued: 94" x 88"; cotton: red, green, pink, yellow and white; hand quilted.

Many women had strong interest in and knowledge of political matters long before they were enfranchised in 1920. The quiltmaker's political preferences are not known, but the Whig party was gaining momentum in the mid 1800s with its proposals advocating a protective tariff and federal control of the currency and banking system. Numerous cotton plantation owners were active in the party and it is not surprising that Whig Rose quilts were popular in the southern states at this time.

Margaret McClure made this vibrant quilt for her sister, Dorcas McClure James. The quilt was brought to Oklahoma Territory before 1900 and has been handed down through three generations of the family.

WORLD WITHOUT END

Maker: Martha Ann Mashburn Ross (1854-1950) and Elisabeth Ellen Mashburn Hancock (1843-1872). Made at Achille, Chickasaw Nation, Indian Territory, circa 1860s.

Owner: Marjorie L. Holley.

Pieced and embroidered: 73" x 64"; wool, silk and cotton: brown, blue and red; not quilted.

The area that is now the state of Oklahoma was not considered an official U.S. Territory at the time of the Civil War. Its early residents were affected, however; for the "Five Civilized Tribes" had been moved here from their land in the southern states and many had owned Negro slaves who came with them. The majority identified with the Confederacy although some Indians were in the Union Army.

Harvey Bacon, grandfather of the two quiltmakers, was a Methodist minister who came from Meridian, Mississippi, when the Chickasaw Indians were moved from that state about 1845. The Bacons settled in Panola which was southeast of what is now the town of Achille, Oklahoma. The family was adopted by the Chickasaw tribe.

Martha Ross and Elisabeth Hancock made this top and did their quilting in the attic of their home in order to keep out of sight of the Union soldiers who came to the territory during the Civil War era.

LOG CABIN, COURTHOUSE STEPS SETTING

Maker: **Eliza Kay (1825-1907). Made in St. Joseph, Missouri, 1890.**

Owner: **Mrs. Harry L. Neuffer, great-granddaughter.**

Pieced: **75" x 63"; wool, silk and satin: black with multi-hues; beaded.**

Silks, satins and the finest fabrics of the period went into this quilt by Mrs. John Kay. The family owned a dry goods store in St. Joseph, Missouri, engaged in outfitting wagons going west. Mrs. Kay regularly went to Philadelphia with her husband on buying trips and thus had access to the newest and best textiles. In addition to being an artist with needlework as indicated with this uniquely beaded quilt, Mrs. Kay also painted china. This exquisite Log Cabin is but one of three striking quilts made by Eliza Kay which were left to her great-granddaughter.

CENTENNIAL ➤

Maker: **Unknown. Probably made at Chicago, Illinois, 1876.**

Owner: **Ruth H. Huskey**

Inscribed: **"1876" in center of quilt.**

Pieced and appliqued: **79" x 76"; cotton: strawberry and cream; hand quilted.**

Quilters frequently commemorate historical events with a quilt design, and this centennial quilt is an excellent example. Superb quilting stitches and workmanship are features of this quilt that has never been washed. It was made as a gift for Emma Clark, who gave it to her daughter, Helen Overton. She brought the quilt to Tulsa, Oklahoma, in 1929.

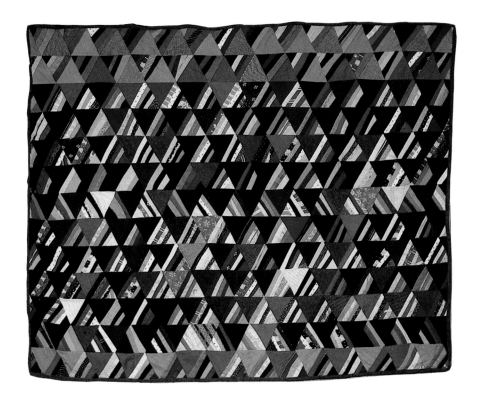

STRING-PIECED PYRAMIDS ∧

Maker: **Gertrude Butler Chadwick (1865-1957). Made at Craig, Missouri, circa 1890.**

Owner: **Eileen C. Kelley.**

Pieced: **79½" x 63"; wool: dark plum and prints; tied.**

People moved from place to place for a variety of reasons, but a major consideration for many families was choosing a locale where their children could attend school. Gertrude and Edgar Chadwick moved to Alva, Oklahoma, just before statehood in 1907 so that their five daughters could attend one of the regional Normal Schools founded to educate teachers in Oklahoma Territory. These schools also provided laboratory classes where students in elementary and high school could receive an education. The move from Missouri was made via train and wagon.

Later, the family moved to Oklahoma City where Mrs. Chadwick was active in the First Methodist Church and was known as an excellent seamstress. Her sparkling Crazy Quilt in the Thousand Pyramids design is made of wool, though silk was the more commonly used fabric for Victorian-era crazy quilts. Mrs. Chadwick's string-pieced pyramids set with very dark solids show a masterful use of light and dark values.

Gertrude Butler Chadwick

S. M. G. Nelson

WHOLE CLOTH WITH TRAPUNTO ⋀

Maker: **Susan Minnie Gleason Nelson (1863-1958). Made in Gillespie, Illinois, 1892.**

Owner: **Greta Sue Jones, great niece.**

Whole cloth: **78" x 62"; cotton: white; hand quilted.**

Designed and made by twenty-nine-year-old, "Susie" Gleason, this superlative quilt won first place in the 1893 World's Columbia Exposition held in Chicago. The elaborate designs on this whole cloth quilt were drawn on the top free-hand, for Susie was not only a master quilter but a talented painter as well. As with many masterpiece quilts brought to Oklahoma, this one was made prior to the quilter's marriage.

Susie Gleason made the Cherokee Strip Land Run by herself, staking claim to farmland near Ames, Oklahoma Territory. There she met and married a young Swedish immigrant, Jonah August Nelson, who had staked claim to a neighboring farm.

"Gus" was the first of his family to leave Sweden for America. Eventually he was able to help his parents, two brothers and three sisters come to the United States, and all lived for a period of time with Susie and Gus until they could establish homes of their own.

* For another quilt by this maker, see "Crazy Quilt", chapter 7, page 123.

"Waiting for the Run, "Guthrie, OK
April 22, 1889
Oklahoma Historical Society photo.

PATRIOTIC COMMEMORATIVE

Maker: Judith Huber Kyler (1857-1933). Made at Ochelata, Washington County, Oklahoma, 1923.

Owner: Betty R. Carter.

Pieced and appliqued: 87" x 66"; cotton: red, white and blue; hand quilted.

In addition to making many quilts for her own family's use, Judith Kyler made them for others. She also operated a hotel in Ochelata. This unique quilt contains forty-eight appliqued stars, representing the men lost in action from Washington County during World War I.

RED CROSS

Maker: Effie Maphet Maxwell (1871-1957). Made at Loyal, Kingfisher County, Oklahoma, 1916-1918.

Owner: Leota Glenn Derrick, daughter.

Pieced: 82" x 80"; cotton: red, white and blue solids; hand quilted.

Effie and her husband Alvin made the land run April 19, 1892, into the Cheyenne and Arapaho Lands and staked a claim. Although the Maxwells were of Irish heritage, most of their neighbors after the Run were immigrants from Germany. The land was flat and rich, ideally suited to raise the hard, red winter wheat as they had done in Europe. The new settlement on the prairie was named Kiel–for the German city from which so many of the residents had come. During World War I, anti-German sentiment ran high and in 1918 the people of Kiel renamed their town "Loyal" to affirm their allegiance to their chosen country, America.

World War I was affecting the Maxwell family of Loyal in another significant way. Their eldest son Johnie was in the service, and Effie made this patriotic–colored quilt while he was serving in the armed forces.

Effie Maphet Maxwell

109

PRESIDENTS

Maker: **Zula Mings Freeman (1893-1969). Made at Arapaho, Custer County, Oklahoma, circa 1935.**

Owner: **Ella Abramson.**

Pieced, appliqued and embroidered: **80" x 66"; cotton: red, white and blue; hand quilted.**

With tiny, even quilting stitches and excellent needle-work skills, Zula Freeman made this patriotic quilt of United States presidents. She and her husband were of German descent, as were their neighbors and close friends, the Kemps. Both had homesteaded, having arrived in Custer County in 1911. This quilt was given to Zula's friend, Hermine Kemp, whom she had assisted at the birth of her daughter, Ella.

STAR

Maker: **Ann Evans John (1844-1922). Made at Carbon, Pittsburg County, Oklahoma, 1917.**

Owner: **Tami Jo Pons, great-granddaughter.**

Pieced and embroidered: **74" x 72"; wool: red and cream; not quilted.**

Born in Wales, Ann Evans John came to the Choctaw Indian Nation about 1884. She was a member of a large family in Wales, but in Oklahoma her family was composed of a mixture of those who were "kin" by blood, marriage and of love. There were cousins from Wales, German relatives from Berlin, plus Scottish-Irish cousins. "Family was family" and she was the center of the clan–the keeper of the history–and it was to her home all seemed to gather in times of happiness and sorrow. She brought many new lives into the world, eased the passing of the old ones, then comforted the ones left behind.

World War I was especially hard on her, because "family" was involved on both sides. She started this quilt in 1917 "so the boys would have a bit of color when they got home." It was kept packed away Christmas of 1917 but brought out after the Armistice of 1918. Not all of the sons, nephews, and cousins represented by the twelve-petal flowers came back from the war. But at a family gathering that armistice year each flower was touched, a name called out, and that man's story told as the quilt hung by the Christmas tree.

Maker: Myrtle Kelley Gandall Cooper (1874-death date unknown). Made in Tulsa, Oklahoma, 1935.

Owner: Collection of the State Museum of History, Oklahoma Historical Society.

Pieced, appliqued and embroidered: 89" x 81"; cotton: red, white and blue; hand quilted.

Caring for the infirm, homeless and aged of society was the responsibility of extended family and neighbors until recent decades. During the Depression years, the number of people needing assistance grew astronomically and various plans were devised to meet their needs. One of these was Dr. Townsend's Old Age Revolving Pension Plan. Proposed in 1934, the plan provided that all citizens of the United States over the age of sixty be paid $200.00 monthly from monies derived from a 2% sales tax. The plan stipulated that the money received by individuals be spent within the month, thus giving momentum to the general economy. A version of the plan was presented to the U.S. House of Representatives in 1939 but was voted down. The plan had many advocates nationwide, and in 1941 a convention of supporters was held in St. Louis with 22,000 delegates in attendance.

Tulsan Myrtle Gandall was a strong proponent of the Townsend Plan and dreamed of making a quilt to honor Dr. Townsend and promote the cause. She had no money to purchase the necessary fabric, so to acquire funds, she participated in a Prosperity Dime Club. Myrtle mailed seven copies of the club's chain letter, a dime in each, to friends across the country. She received sixty-five dimes through the chain–enough to purchase materials for her quilt.

Each part of the original design had significance and symbolism to the quiltmaker and she wrote a booklet about her quilt called "When Our Dreams Come True." A nationwide Social Security system came into being rather than Dr. Townsend's Plan, but quiltmaker Myrtle Gandall Cooper had recorded a bit of history in her quilt for posterity.

WORLD'S FAIR FABRIC ➤

Maker: Pearl E. Davis McCutchan (1898-1976). Made in Tonkawa, Kay County, Oklahoma, 1939.

Owner: Berniece McCutchan Pyle, daughter.

Whole cloth: 85" x 67"; cotton: multi-hued print; tied.

A relatively small percentage of Oklahoma women had opportunity to travel widely prior to World War II. The McCutchan family was living in Tonkawa, Oklahoma, in 1939. Their daughter Marie, who loved traveling to places of historical interest, decided to attend the World's Fair in New York City. When she returned, she shared many memories of her trip.

Her sister Berniece saw in the downtown Oklahoma City Montgomery Ward department store, a bolt of fabric that depicted exhibits at the fair. Because she had heard her sister tell about the event, she bought some yardage. Berniece had never made a quilt so her mother agreed to make it for her. The quilt will be left to Berniece Pyle's nephew, Charles Kuzniar, since it was his mother's World Fair trip which inspired it.

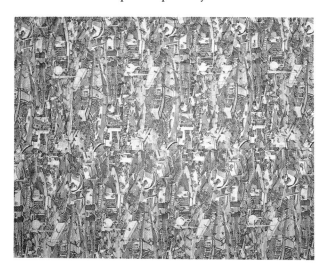

Pearl Davis McCutchan

SNOW WHITE AND THE SEVEN DWARFS

Maker: **Billie Newton Menifee (1915-   ). Quilter unknown. Made in Oklahoma City, Oklahoma, 1939.**

Owner: **Joyce Menifee, daughter-in-law.**

Inscribed: **"Walt Disney."**

Appliqued and embroidered: **55" x 39"; cotton: white background; hand quilted.**

Movies were a popular entertainment during the 1930s. When Billie Menifee was expecting her first child, she made this delightful quilt top and sent it to the Walt Disney Studio in California for his autograph. His signature was embroidered to preserve it. The baby born was a son, James Calvin Menifee. He married Joyce and in 1967 when she was expecting her first child, her mother-in-law presented the quilt to her as a special gift at a baby shower.

EMBROIDERED SAMPLER   ❯

Maker: **Emma Kluting Clampitt Rock (1857-1938). Made near Coalgate, Coal County, Oklahoma, 1908.**

Owner: **Clara Mildred Clampitt Moree.**

Embroidered: **77" x 68"; cotton: multi-colored thread on white; hand quilted.**

A great variety of designs including leap year, farm scenes, initials, some original and some traditional patterns appear in this embroidered sampler made by Emma Rock.

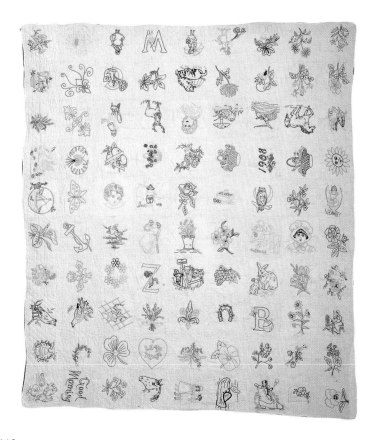

Chalitso Club, Clinton, Oklahoma. 1933

MITCHELL QUILT ❯

Maker: **Chalitso Club. Made in Clinton, Custer County, Oklahoma, 1933.**

Owner: **Mrs. Bernice Mitchell Peace.**

Inscribed: **"Mitchell for Governor–Chalitso Club, Clinton, Oklahoma, 1933."**

Embroidered: **98" x 90"; cotton: rose; hand quilted.**

Oklahoma became the forty-sixth state in the Union in 1907 and Guthrie was the state capitol. In 1910, the capitol was moved to Oklahoma City and E.L. Mitchell was part of the group responsible for this controversial act. He was active in public service and political activities, ranging from serving as a member of the local school board and city mayor to State Senator and Corporation Commissioner. In 1933, he was one of the Democratic candidates vying for role as the party's nominee for governor. Ernest W. Marland was selected instead and became governor in 1935.

The people of Clinton expressed their sentiments and pride in their native son by making a quilt promoting his candidacy. Designed by Mrs. C.R. Summers, sixteen women made blocks and embroidered their names in black under a state flower. The Chalitso Club also did the quilting and proudly posed with their finished project. The center features an actual photograph of Mr. Mitchell and the corners have the insignia of the National Recovery Act, a program designed to help end the Depression.

ORIGINAL-- TILLIE THE TOILER

Maker: Merle Guinn Thompson (1910-1976). Made in Graham, Texas, 1928-1930.

Owner: J. Alton Thompson

Pieced: 84" x 66"; cotton: rose and green; drawn with India ink; hand quilted.

Truly a unique gem, this quilt top was designed and made by Merle Guinn while a student at Texas Women's College (now Texas Wesleyan) in Fort Worth. Across town at Texas Christian University, the young man who was later to become her husband was a student also, and he recalls her work on this quilt. She selected the color scheme and collected pictures of "Tillie the Toiler" from the newspaper, then started drawing the designs in India ink. Two years later when the blocks were complete, Merle worked with her mother to set the blocks together and do the quilting.

In 1934, Merle married her college sweetheart, Alton Thompson, and both taught in Texas. In 1939 they moved to Frederick, Oklahoma, where they operated the Frederick Florist for twenty-eight years. The quiltmaker made about twenty quilts during her lifetime.

APPLIQUED POPPIES

Maker: Clara Spangler Andrews (1868-1950). Made in Vinita, Craig County, Oklahoma, 1932.

Owner: Roberta J. Bagby, granddaughter.

Appliqued: 94" x 72"; cotton: red and green on ecru; hand quilted.

An example of the 1930s floral applique style which evolved from Art Nouveau designs of previous decades, this Applique Poppy was a published design which none but the most skilled quiltmakers attempted. Floral designs of all types–pieced, appliqued and embroidered–were a hallmark of this period. Whether life-like, as in Mrs. Andrews' Applique Poppies, or highly stylized and abstract, floral patterns were created by thousands of quiltmakers, perhaps to add bright notes of cheer to families hard hit by the economic downturn.

Chapter VII

ARTWORK

Art comes in many forms, but at its best gives the artist a means of self expression. Through many decades, needlework skills were deemed an important part of every girl's education and there was acclaim for exquisite workmanship. Just being able to make the stitches perfectly was not enough for many, however, and they found an outlet for their creativity in the choice of color and in creating their own designs. Their artifacts met the criteria of being quilts for they were three layers held together with stitches, but they were also art using fabric and thread as the medium.

Oklahoma Sunburst

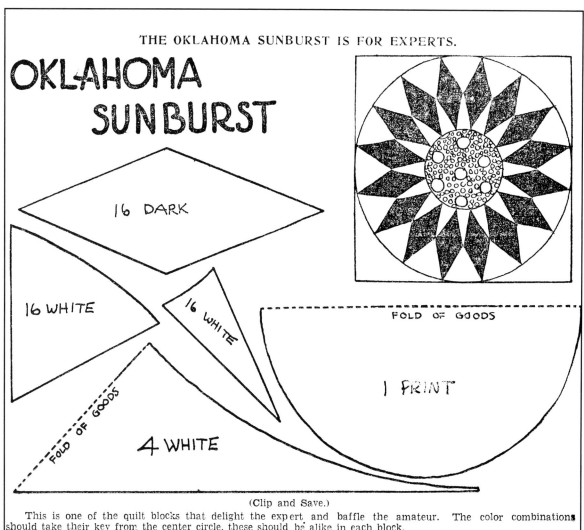

THE OKLAHOMA SUNBURST IS FOR EXPERTS.

OKLAHOMA SUNBURST

16 DARK

16 WHITE

16 WHITE

FOLD OF GOODS

4 WHITE

FOLD OF GOODS

1 PRINT

(Clip and Save.)

This is one of the quilt blocks that delight the expert and baffle the amateur. The color combinations should take their key from the center circle, these should be alike in each block.

◀ ORIGINAL TREE OF LIFE

Maker: **Sarah Bennington Rickett (1835-1915). Made in Chula, Missouri, 1898.**

Owner: Ila Rickett Fry.

Appliqued and embroidered: **82" x 88"; cotton: green, pink, black and gold; hand quilted.**

With an artist's eye, Sarah Rickett designed and made this quilt for her son Edward's twenty-first birthday. Testament to the maker's profound love of nature, the quilt is bursting with life—the tree wants to grow right off the quilt! From the tree's flowing branches spring flowers, hearts and birds. The Tree of Life is framed by a trailing grapevine border.

This quilt alone would be an impressive accomplishment for any quiltmaker, but Sarah was the mother of ten children and made an original, appliqued quilt for each. In addition to her own ten, she also took in twelve more children whose parents had died. A granddaughter said of Sarah Rickett, "She always had a quilt in the frame and another one in the piecing stage."

This beautiful example of quilt art came to Oklahoma Territory in 1901 with Sarah's son.

FOLDED LOG CABIN ▶

Maker: Ciacha Elizabeth Hood Ballard (1866-1952). Made in Ottawa or Delaware County, Oklahoma, circa 1920.

Owner: Jo Lee Ballard Faulkner, granddaughter.

Pieced: 78" x 66"; silk, satin, taffeta: multicolors with black; not quilted.

The colors glow in this quilt top made of silk, crepe, satin and tafetta by Ciacha Ballard. She was born at Echo in Indian Territory on land that is now under water off Monkey Island in Grand Lake O' the Cherokees. She was a white woman married to a half-blood Cherokee, and their lives were spent in far northeastern Oklahoma.

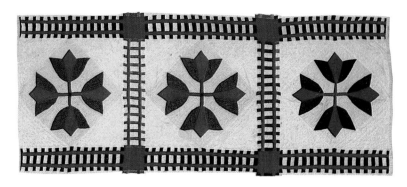

DUTCH TULIP ∧

Maker: **Sarah Alice Workman Shaw (1870-1957). Made at Buffalo Valley, Pushmataha County, Indian Territory, circa 1900.**

Owner: **Catherine Gail Fassino.**

Pieced: **70" x 69"; cotton: red and green on white; hand quilted.**

While the flower design is traditional, the intricately pieced sashing between the blocks is most unique.

Sarah Workman Shaw

Sarah Pruitt

SUNFLOWER WITH VINING BUDS ❭

Maker: **Sarah Hicks Marshall Pruitt (c. 1827-1888). Made in Arkansas or Indian Territory, circa 1875-1885.**

Owner: **June Cornwell Stone, great-great granddaughter.**

Appliqued and pieced: **74" x 59"; cotton: brown, gold, cream and green; hand quilted.**

Truly an artist with fabric, Sarah Pruitt made this quilt toward the end of her lifetime after she was widowed for the second time. Some of the fabric appears to be home dyed, and it is quite possible that she may have created her own original pattern for this heirloom.

118

OKLAHOMA HISTORY QUILT

Maker: Camille Nixdorf Phelan (1882-d. date unknown). Made in Oklahoma City, Oklahoma, 1935.

Inscribed: "Camille Nixdorf Phelan 1935."

Owner: Collection of the State Museum of History, Oklahoma Historical Society.

Embroidered: 93" x 76½"; cotton: multi-colored thread on grey with green border; hand quilted.

Two years of research and four of sewing resulted in this embroidered history of Oklahoma by Camille Nixdorf Phelan. This extraordinarily detailed pictorial quilt contains realistic renderings of prominent citizens and events, historic buildings, and native flora and fauna. The quilt is described as "One of the most unique of all state quilts" on Page 39 of *The Romance of the Patchwork Quilt* by Hall and Kretsinger.

The quiltmaker, a Missouri native, was educated at St Joseph's Academy, St. Louis, where she received her art instruction. Camille and Dr. J.R. Phelan were married in 1900; they moved to Oklahoma City in 1901.

Though embroidery was her favorite hobby, Mrs. Phelan succumbed to the lure of quilting, then a popular pastime across America. To best utilize her own talents, she decided to create an embroidered record of her state's historical personages, along with events of significance. It was the quiltmaker's opinion that "in most of the published records...the sordid and rough element has been exploited to the exclusion of the cultural and artistic." Mrs. Phelan created this quilt expressly for donation to the Oklahoma Historical Society.

She describes the process thus: " In actual making, I first selected the pictures I wanted to reproduce, then I carefully sketched a replica on the cloth, reducing or enlarging it as was required to fit the space assigned it, then it was roughly outlined with black silk thread in order to give it an outstanding effect. With needle and thread I then carefully worked in the expression . . . The work was protected by a cellophane covering until the retouching of high lights was finished. This was done with soft tinted thread as an artist uses his retouching brush on canvas. After all the figures were finished, the quilting was done. Twenty 100-yard spools of thread were used."

Records in the Oklahoma Historical Society list every pictorial element on the quilt and the role it played in the state's history.

LONE STAR ❯

Maker: Mrs. Ballard. Made in St. Louis, Missouri, circa 1850-1875.

Owner: Agnes Leonard Roberts.

Pieced: 84" x 84"; cotton: multi-colors with green and white border; hand quilted.

This beautiful quilt was made in the third quarter of the 19th century and came to Oklahoma in 1930 as a special gift to the maker's daughter, Edith Ballard Scott. Mrs. Scott lived in Muskogee, Oklahoma, and was affectionately known as "Scottie."

Creating a single Lone Star design is challenging but this nameless quiltmaker added four additional stars, each composed of minute diamonds. The quilt is a gem!

❮ BUSY HANDS

Maker: Unknown. Made in Sevier County, Arkansas, circa 1890.

Owner: James E. and Dorothy P. Floyd.

Appliqued and pieced: 78½" x 68"; cotton: feed sacks and cretonne–blues and browns; hand quilted.

Named Busy Hands by the family, this whimsical example of African/American folk art was made by a Negro woman who worked for the Newton Perry Floyd family in Arkansas. Her name was not recorded, but it is known that she made it for the family's son, Robert Anders Floyd. In 1912, he and his wife moved with the quilt to Bryan County, Oklahoma. It has been quilted in recent years by family members.

STRING PIECED BLOCKS ⌄

Maker: Caroline "Callie" Hyden Wilmoth (1853-1941). Made near Idabel, Choctaw Nation, Indian Territory, circa 1900.

Owner: Ruth Cherokee Young, granddaughter.

Pieced: 68" x 64"; cotton: red and blue prints and solids; hand quilted.

Callie Hyden was a child during the Civil War but remembered it vividly, recounting many memories for her children and grandchildren. She also recalled riding sidesaddle beside her father, Dr. William T. Hyden, as he made rounds doctoring the sick in Johnson County, Arkansas. The family moved about 1880 to Indian Territory where Dr. Hyden served as doctor for the Choctaw tribe in Pushmataha County.

It is not known how many quilts Callie made but this vivid quilt shows her love of color.

Callie Wilmoth (seated) & family

‹ **MARINER'S COMPASS WITH EIGHT-POINTED STAR**

Maker: **Nancy Martin Hanna (c. 1870-1908). Made in Arkansas, circa 1885.**

Owner: **Mrs. Glenda Arnhart.**

Pieced: **80" x 77"; cotton: navy, yellow, green; wool batting; hand quilted.**

Quiltmaker Nancy Martin Hanna was of Irish descent, and family history relates that this original Mariner's Compass was made about the time of her marriage at age fifteen. Mrs. Hanna's adept use of tonal values gives a feeling of depth to her design. By using the purest color in the center of each block, the eight-pointed stars glow with a golden light.

This talented quiltmaker not only had an eye for design but excellent quilting skills that she utilized in creating beautiful shells with her stitches. The quilt has been handed down through several generations of the family after coming to the Mangum area of Oklahoma Territory before the turn of the century.

MARINER'S COMPASS--LOST SHIP SETTING ›

Maker: **Minerva Jane Potter Vincent (1854-1933). Made in Missouri, circa 1900.**

Owner: **Ellen Vincent Husky, granddaughter.**

Pieced: **86" x 74"; cotton: multi-colors with gold, blue and brown; hand quilted.**

Minerva Jane Vincent made many quilts in her lifetime, but this one was completed about the time of her husband's death. Left with six children to rear, Minerva was supported by her son, James–only fourteen–who worked for the railroad in Kansas. In 1904, the family moved to a farm in Grant County, Oklahoma Territory.

Minerva Potter Vincent

121

Sarah Eismann Ransom & family

SIX–POINTED STAR ❯

Maker: Sarah Ellen Eismann Ransom (1853-1937). Made in Pennsylvania, circa 1865.

Owner: Mrs. N.F. Inciardi, granddaughter.

Pieced: 72½" x 70"; cotton: red, green and white; wool batting; hand quilted.

Not only did this quiltmaker achieve a new look with her block arrangement but the choice of color creates an entirely different dimension than traditional quilts made of six-pointed stars. Sarah Ransom made this treasure early in her life and brought it with the family's possessions when they came to the Pond Creek area of Grant County well before the turn of the century.

TOBACCO PLANT

Maker: Linnie Russel Wilder (1854-1884). Made in Naples, Texas, before 1884.

Owner: Wynonah Thomas, granddaughter.

Appliqued and pieced: 83" x 69"; cotton: green, brown and gold; hand quilted.

Quiltmaker Linnie Russel Wilder died at age thirty; but her widower, Sam Wilder, and son, Orville Wilder, kept the Tobacco Plant quilt she had made and brought it with them when they came to Haileyville, Choctaw Nation, Indian Territory, in 1903.

Though this quilt is known by the family as Tobacco Plant, it bears similarities to a 19th century floral design called "Egyptian Lotus."

❮ LONE STAR

Maker: Minnie Roberts Mitchell (1884-1965); Made at Valliant, McCurtain County, Oklahoma, 1920-1925.

Owner: Alma Mitchell Bain, daughter.

Pieced: 72" x 64"; cotton: red, green, gold and beige; hand quilted.

The current owner of this dramatic quilt says, "This quilt was mother's pride and joy. It was used as a decorative piece not as a cover for warmth." Obviously, Minnie Roberts Mitchell had an eye for color, and home dyed some of the fabric with tree bark and berries to achieve the shades needed for this masterpiece. Minnie made the batting herself: picking the cotton from what was left in the field, taking it to the gin for cleaning, and carding by hand to form batts of the desired thickness.

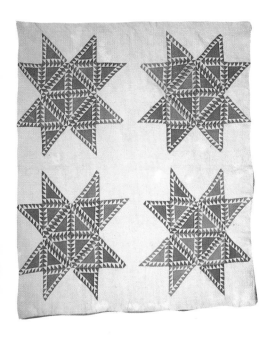

STAR SPANGLED BANNER

Maker: Unknown. Probably made in West Virginia, circa 1900.

Owner: Sarah E. Caylor.

Pieced: 85" x 70"; cotton: red, white, and blue; hand quilted.

Although the quiltmaker's name is not known, the maker was obviously a skilled artist in fabric for each of the four blocks contains 639 pieces precisely stitched together. This design is one of the most intricate of any "feathered star" type.

The Star Spangled Banner quilt was brought to Oklahoma City in the 1920s by the family of Warren J. Martin, a petroleum land broker. Daughter Marjory Martin Caylor later gave the quilt to her daughter-in-law.

STRING PIECED STAR ❯

Maker: Dreda LeFlore (1895-   ).
Quilted by Mrs. Bryan Wingfield. Made at Buffalo Head, Atoka County, Oklahoma, 1918.

Owner: Mamie Ballew.

Pieced: 84" x 68"; Cotton: red and blue; hand quilted.

Working with bits and pieces of calico, Dreda LeFlore created this colorful design by hand piecing onto newspaper. Extra star blocks have been saved, and a poem titled "Knitting Socks" is printed on the newspaper backing that speaks of World War I activities.

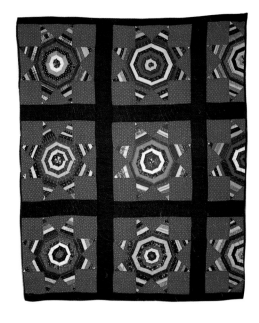

CRAZY QUILT

Maker: Susan Minnie Gleason Nelson (1863-1958). Made in Ames, Major County, Oklahoma, 1893-1908.

Owner: Nettie E. Nelson Crawford, daughter.

Appliqued, pieced, embroidered: 88" x 72"; velvet and silk: multi-hues; corded facing; not quilted.

Lovely embroidery work and painted designs make this quilt distinctive. It was started before 1893 when Susan Gleason was in Illinois and completed after she staked a claim in Oklahoma territory, September 16, 1893.

For this quilt Susan exchanged pieces of fabric by mail. Each state of the United States plus some islands are represented. Included are pieces of dresses that belonged to the wives of three presidents–Lincoln, Grant and Cleveland. Another scrap was from a daughter of President Cleveland.

*For further family history and another quilt by this maker, see "Whole Cloth with Trapunto," Chapter 6, page 108.

123

VARIABLE STAR WITH ORIGINAL APPLIQUE

Maker: Gertrude Truesdale. Made in Wisconsin, circa 1815.

Owner: Marjorie J. Reese, great-granddaughter.

Pieced, appliqued, embroidered: 86" x 80"; cotton: red and white; hand quilted.

    Personal symbolism abounds in the applique motifs of Gertrude Truesdale's Variable Star quilt. In addition to traditional heart and star designs, the maker included tracings of her children's hands, drawings of family pets and abundant botanical forms from her gardens. Called Double Star by the family, this highly personalized example of folk art at its finest is effectively framed by a charming bow and swag border.
    Made in Wisconsin early in the last century, the quilt was brought to Lawton, Oklahoma, in 1906 by the maker's granddaughter, Grace Gertrude Armitage Puttkamer.

FEDERAL EAGLE QUILT

Maker: Anna Catharine Hummel Markey Garnhart (1773-1860). Made in Frederick, Maryland, 1820.

Owner: Plains Indians and Pioneers Museum, Woodward, Oklahoma.

Appliqued: 94" x 91"; cotton: green, black, gold and white; hand quilted.

Anna Catharine Garnhart was born of German immigrants in Frederick, Maryland. In addition to being a skilled quiltmaker, Anna was a gifted healer or herb doctor. She learned to use native plants and herbs from the Indians of the area.

The eagle quilt pictured is one of three made by Anna, and another of which is owned by the D.A.R. Museum, Washington, D.C. The eagle in the quilt is similar to the one in the Great Seal of the United States, but it has reverse applique feathers rather than a shield on its breast. It is possible that the many leaves and fruits in the designs were used by Anna in her herbal medicine. She made the quilt using the reverse applique technique which meant the top fabric was cut out in the chosen pattern, the print material placed beneath, and tiny blanket stitches held the two pieces in place. Anna probably made the thread herself.

The quilt was given to the museum in 1966.

TIT FOR TAT ❯

Maker: Ella L. Geers Veach (1855-1933). Made at Lexington, Kentucky, 1931.

Owner: Monte and Margie Dodson, great-nephew.

Pieced: 95" x 74"; cotton: multi-color scraps and white; hand quilted.

This family treasure designed with tiny triangles was made in Kentucky by Ella Veach shortly before here death and left to her sister in Oklahoma. The quiltmaker had another quilt under construction and it included some of the same pieces of fabric, along with her intact needle. Obviously, Ella's collection of "scraps" was like an artist's palette; and in her hands, the humble scrap quilt is elevated to a work of art.

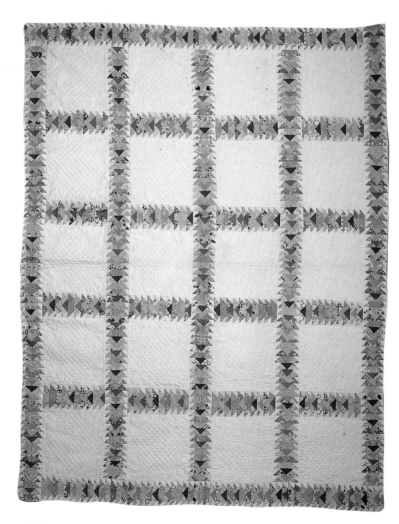

SUNBURST MEDALLION

Maker: **Mother of Mary Piner Offutt. Made in Kansas, circa 1875-1900.**

Owner: **Shirlene Swan (Mrs. Roger).**

Pieced: **88" x 87"; cotton: assorted prints in tones of brown, gold, rust and white; wool batting; hand quilted, 12 stitches to the inch.**

Little is known about the maker of this magnificent quilt, except that she was a Kansas resident and of German descent. Mrs. Piner gave the quilt to her daughter, Mary, prior to her marriage to Joseph Offutt. The quilt was brought to Oklahoma City sometime between 1910 and 1920. As Mary had no children, the quilt was given to the present owner because of her love for quilts.

A museum piece in every sense, called Mariner's Compass by the family, the design consists of a center medallion plus twelve blocks surrounding. Each sunburst has 24 points composed of hundreds of tiny diamond-shaped pieces. The sashing is of pieced diamonds, and there are seven outer borders framing the design. The quilt is in superb condition and has never been washed.

EPILOGUE

Quilts continued to be made in Oklahoma after 1940 and those reflect the impact of World War II, the advent of synthetic fabrics sometimes blended with cotton, the revival of interest in quilting as the nation prepared to celebrate the bicentennial, unparalleled tools, books, magazines, and supplies made available for quiltmakers in the 1980s--but that is another story. Future quilt lovers will be able, with the perspective of time, to tell that story more objectively than we. They will add another chapter to the ongoing saga of quilts that began in Asia, traveled to Europe in the middle ages, arrived on the American continent with the first colonial families, and now can be found on every continent of the globe. Quilts will continue to provide warmth for the physical body, beauty for the soul, and provide a delightful reflection of the people who make, use and cherish them.

OKLAHOMA QUILT DAY REGISTRATION

The nineteen QUILT DAY registrations were a free public service and took place in libraries, community centers, churches, historical houses, fairground buildings, and schools. Often, people were lined up with their quilts waiting for the opening hour. At the entrance each quilt was assigned an identification number and the owner received a duplicate as proof of ownership.

Some people brought family records and photographs to use as they filled out the questionnaire. Frequently several generations of a family came together and spent considerable time discussing the lineage and dates pertinent to the quilt's history. A few people hurried through this important process but most gave careful consideration to what would be recorded for posterity about their quilt's maker. Numerous people discovered additonal facts after the QUILT DAY and mailed that information so that it could be added to their quilt's registration form. As people reflected on their family history, several expressed the sentiment, "Grandmother would be so pleased to know that her quilt is being registered and that her story will be remembered."

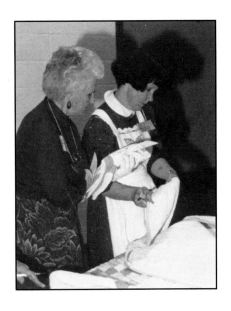

Quilts were handled with white gloves as they were measured and prepared for being photographed. Taking pictures of quilts requires special equipment and handling procedures. Portable, plastic racks were designed for use in this project.

Most quilts were attached to a rod with clips and the quilt carefully lifted into position for about one minute so that photos could be taken. Some quilts were too fragile to be hung and those were placed on white sheets on the floor.

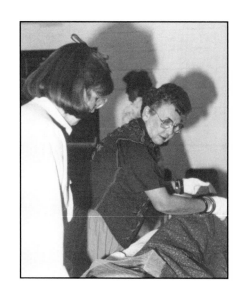

Colored slides of each quilt will be placed in the archives of the Oklahoma Historical Society along with the data on the questionnaire. Instant developing color film was used for a secondary photo of each quilt and these pictures were attached to the quilt form for visual identification.

Careful, detailed examination of each quilt was time consuming but an essential part of the process. Relying on reference books in addition to their own extensive knowledge of quilt patterns and textiles, evaluators recorded specific data about the quilting techniques and fabrics used. Their notes about fabric age and pattern identification were written on the quilt's form and on a paper given to the owner. Some quilt owners knew a great deal about their artifact when they arrived, for a detailed history had been passed along with the quilt; but others came to the registration day just hoping to learn the name of their quilt's pattern and were delighted to also discover the age of the fabric. In a number of instances, the age of the fabric provided the clue needed for family members to determine which generation of ancestors had made the quilt.

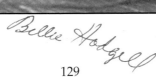

Periodically during the day, an informative talk was given to the audience about how families can effectively document and record quilt legacy memories for future generations. Participants were encouraged to keep vintage quilts within the family unit and to deliberately help other relatives understand and appreciate these heirlooms. Advice was given on proper care and storage of vintage textiles.

Quilts were returned at the site after ownership was verified through the identification system. Each participant received a care leaflet and a certificate indicating that the heirloom had been part of the Oklahoma QUILT DAY registration project.

In addition to the traveling team members at each of the nineteen locations, numerous local volunteers assisted in the massive undertaking of processing up to 325 quilts in one day.

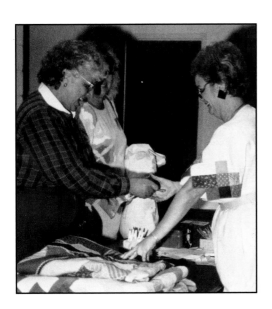

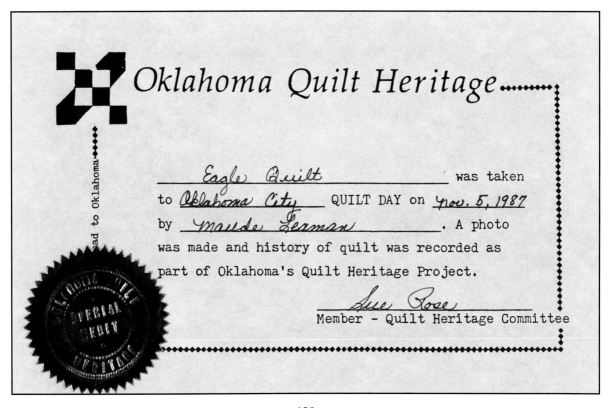

Oklahoma Quilt Heritage........

_____Eagle Quilt_____ was taken to _Oklahoma City_ QUILT DAY on _nov. 5, 1987_ by _maude Leaman_. A photo was made and history of quilt was recorded as part of Oklahoma's Quilt Heritage Project.

Sue Rose
Member - Quilt Heritage Committee

OKLAHOMA QUILT DAY SITES AND VOLUNTEERS

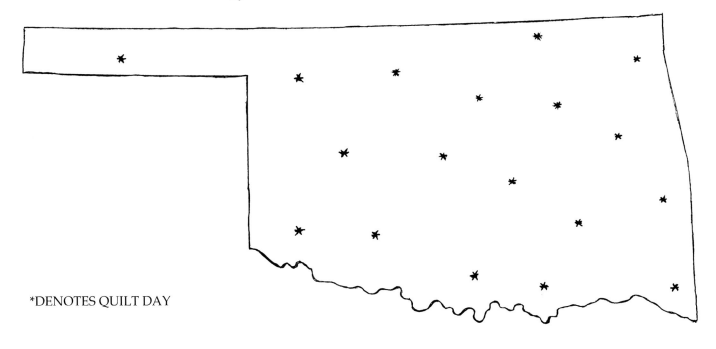

*DENOTES QUILT DAY

THE TRAVELING TEAM WORKED THE 19 QUILT DAYS ACROSS THE STATE

Jane Amstutz Harnden
Pamela Frazee Woolbright
Trudy Mitchell Gullo
Betty Jo Schroder Haines
Thelma Hill Baker

Patricia Duerksen Higgins
Susanne Sanford Rose
Lorraine Moore Lear
Bille Seward Hodgell
Jeri-Alynn Rhoads McGee

---

*Altus. . .May 17, 1988. . .St. Paul's Episcopal Church. . .Mona Boyd, local coordinator

Sponsor: Southwest Oklahoma Quilters Guild

Mamie Ashley	Jo Fancher	Margaret Martin	Marie Sheraden
Terri Bloomberg	Connie Gilliam	Opal Nell McAlexander	Helen Tate
Pat Cutis	Jean Hestand	Ella McDaniels	Sandi Thomas
Lola Davis	Renee Howard	Marilyn Nicholls	Norene Todd
Mary Dollar	Jackie Hubert	Ruth Puley	Gladys Winn
Ida Mae Drury	Velma Lawrence	Sally Rising	Ida Fay Winters
Lisa Drury			Lisa Worrell

*Ardmore. . . June 28, 1988. . .St. Phillip's Episcopal Church. . .Jane Tuttle, local coordinator
Sponsor: Southern Oklahoma Quilters Guild

Irene Ayers	Ruth Ann McCollum
Pauline Bray	Helen McCurry
June Busby	Lennie McCurry
Marie Colvert	Ann Pretty
Arline Guthary	Dorothy Riley
Renaee Hoyle	Nancy Smalley
Annie Lemay	Anna Stracener
Ora Lemons	Leta Faye Wilkins

*<u>Bartlesville</u>. . .August 11, 1987. . .Community Center. . .Ruth Montgomery, local coordinator
Sponsor: Jubilee Quilters Guild

Velma Anderson	Ruth Cozad	Nancy Klahn	Lucille Powell
Verena Beazer	Diane Davis	Carla Korthase	Shari Preszler
Clois Benge	Lou Edmonds	Cheryl Lansdown	Dortha Shorter
Jeannie Bennett	Meg Greenwood	Debby Lee	Lela Stevenson
Lavina Berner	June Grissom	Dorothy McBurney	Sandy Test
Ethel Burleigh	Charlotte Hawkins	Jan McCracken	Grace Young
Annette S. Copeland	Barbara Hoffman	Nettie Parker	

*<u>Clinton</u>. . . October 10, 1987. . . Senior Citizen's Center. . .Janet Bonny, local coordinator
Sponsor: Western Oklahoma Quilters Guild

Darlene Badgett	Juanita Jincks	Judy Reeder	Jadla Vaught
Judy Beyer	Patty Kennemur	Jo Ann Robinson	Eleanore Waggoner
Dortha Clay	Billie Ruth	Marable Cecilia Schneburger	Gail Wilcox
Evelyn Hart	Lenore Marcy	Mary Shank	Jodie Williams
Beula Isch	E.M. Millspaugh	Linda Travis	

*<u>Durant</u>. . .March 28,1988 . . . First Presbyterian Church . . .Sara Person, local coordinator
Sponsor: Three Valley Museum

Mary Baskin	Winona Harrison	Charlene Lantz	Juanita K. Thomas
Cherokee Rose Carter	Dorothy Hicks	Bozetta McClindon	Jo Tucker
Ruth Cherokee	Calvin Holley	Mary Claude Park	Ann Vaughan
Dorothy Clay	Marjorie Holley	Paula Platter	Betty Wakefield
Virginia Dodd	Becky Husan	Dixie Prater	Leslie Webster
Bill Dodd	Ray Julian	Royce Prentice	Ruby Wilson
Janet Fernandez	Ross Kirven	Mildred Scoggins	Joyce Wixom
Jerhee Foote	Ed Knight	Sarah Jane Seeley	Susan Wright
Dorothy Gumm	Julia Knight	Deborah Smith	

*<u>Enid</u> . . .October 24,1988. . . Enid Mennonite Brethren Church . . . Arba Jo Pope and Lillie Momsen, local coordinators
Sponsor: Garfield County Extension Homemakers Council

Bertha Adams	Wynona Kuhnemund	Elizabeth Reiger	Irene Squires
Nancy Buckminster	Jakita Miiller	Faye Riffel	Sophia Thesman
Dorothy Cozart	Bettye Phillips	Hope Russell	Helen Toews
Sue Erickson	Carol Posey	Christine Schiltz	Kay Toews
Irene Green	Angelina Pribil	Ada Schmitz	Ann Warkentin
			Mildred Zahb

*<u>Goodwell</u>. . . June 14, 1988. . . No Man's Land Museum. . . Joan Kachel, local coordinator
Sponsor: No Man's Land Historical Society

Jane Burton	Johnita Glocen	Mary A. Kelley	Renee Pearson
Johnie L. Davis	Gaynell Henderson	Mary Ann Mayer	Barbara Rohlander
Carla Farrand	Heath Holmes	Leo McMakin	Mary Lea Sample
Joyce Fischer	Vernon L. Hopson	Jill Morrison	
Joy Foreman	Becky Hopson	Mary Olsen	

*<u>Grove</u>. . . August 30, 1988. . . Community Center. . . Edna Mae Phillips, local coordinator
Sponsor: Grand Lakes O' the Cherokees Quilt Guild

Marion Barrier	Marguerite "Maggie" Fraser	Verna Painter	Doris Selvidge
Eva Betzor	Nina Frazier	Mayme Poe	Eleanor Snell
Joanne Bickel	Lola Garrison	Elaine Proctor	Margaret Summers
Dorothy Clark	Luceil Graham	Gloria Richardson	Maxine Voth
Helen Dessert	Marie Hamlett	Betty Robertson	Harriet Meadors Wheeler
Lorene Dougherty	Allis Jerrems	Virginia Secor	Florence Winn
Elsie Foreman			Norma Zaldo

*<u>Idabel</u>. . . October 11, 1988. . . Barnes-Stevenson House. . . Trilla Frazier and Ruby Harris, local coordinators
Sponsor: McCurtain County Historical Society

Bobbie Anderson	Jo Frazier	Lavonda Reeves	Pat Talbot
Eva Briley	Linda Greene	Betty Sasser	Betty Vedder
Lynda Coffin	Pennie Mixon	Georgia Smith	Inez Wade
Katherine Flowers	Leona Neuendor	Patsy Stevens	Bonnie Waldrop
			Sheryl Ward

*<u>Lawton</u>. . . May 19, 1988. . . Center for Creative Living. . . Jo Hollye Silvers, local coordinator
Sponsor: Kiamichi Quilters Guild and Piece Makers Quilt Guild

E. Marie Brewer	Bernice Dennis	Billie Ruth Lycan	Doris Rightmer
Marlies Burdine	Bessie Doane	Alize Nation	Sharon Shadburn
Jackie Canfield	Doris Eilderts	Katherine Rayl	Hazel Stephens
Anncliose Collins	Freida Gates	Thelma Regan	Lorraine Stephens
			Helen Wolf

*<u>McAlester</u>. . . May 11, 1988. . . Cafeteria of Old High School. . . Alice Thompson, local coordinator
Sponsor: Kiamichi Quilters Guild and Piece Makers Quilt Guild

Mary Bridgewater	Lou Green	Oneta Martin	Joyce R. Shannon
Carol Bryant	Ann Hackett	Norma Meuser	Golda Smith
Bobbie J. Cooper	Janice Hamilton	Delores Nickerson	Betty Speligene
Elouise DeGiaconio	Helen R. Haynes	Sue Overton	Rose M. Stoos
Kathaleen DeLana	Sherron Hiarad	Rosa Pollock	Alea Thompson
Mary Ann Gaherinn	Mary Ann Kreager	Faye Pursley	Ida Mae West
Joanna Grant			Mary Wright

*<u>Muskogee</u>. . . Novenber 9, 1988. . . Public Library. . . Jean Haynes, local coordinator

Susanne Auten	Barbara Green	Ella Ragsdale	Alice L. Ward
Faye Deane Boydstun	Oda Hammons	Reba Scherer	Katie Wilson
Ruth Brady	Delores Nickerson	Elinor Self	Wilma Woods
Wanda Burton	Anne Pringle	Shirley Vedder	MaryJane Youngblood
Lisa Esterline			Morris Youngblood

*<u>Oklahoma City, North</u>. . . November 5, 1987. . . St. Augustine of Canterbury Episcopal Church. . .
Pam Woolbright, local coordinator. . . Sponsor: Central Oklahoma Quilter Guild

Sue Anthony	Dottie Doughty	Nettie Martin	Roberta Reubell
Candy Antonio	Beverly Estlinbaum	Margaret McWilliams	Vesta Nadine Robertson
Norma Brandeberry	Inez Frame	Vicki Medlin	Barbara Russell
Mary Bugelholl	Glenna Hailey	Mildred Moodie	Polly Stewart
Crista Bushman	Pam Hainer	Jeanie Moore	Robie Stewart
Debbie Davis	Lydia Kennemann	Carmen Mosca	Beulah Ward
Joan Dobber	Rhoda Libitz	Thelma Petty	Linda Williams

*<u>Oklahoma City, South</u> . . . April 12, 1988 . . . Antioch Christian Church . . . Judy Butts, local coordinator. . .
Sponsor: Central Oklahoma Quilters Guild

Glenda Argo	Arlene Ferik	Sidney Lowery	Lois Small
Lura Ayling	Mary Gassaway	Pat Merrill	Judy Start
Corinne Beck	Charlene Gilmore	Jeanie Moore	Polly Stewart
Mary Bugelhall	Carolyn Hays	Elizabeth Oliver	Saundra Swinny
June Calvert	Ann Huffman	Dianna Parrish	Laura Thomas
Henrietta Cross	Kathye Johnson	Dorothy Jean Peach	Opal Thompson
Evelyn Day	Evelyn Lewis	Christine Pryor	Ellamay Weuste
Mabel Dossie	Rhoda Libez	Nancy Shepard	

*<u>Poteau</u> . . . September 27, 1988 . . . Kidd Community Center . . . Belle Zuck, local coordinator . . .
Sponsor: Poteau Pearls Extension Homemakers and Mountaindale Quilting Club

Betty Brundige	Virginia Neff
Helen Files	Polly Scatterfield
Mabel Frizzell	Dora Small
Florence Goins	Rose Vangorder
Velma Gregory	Ruby Walden
Ruth Luman	Betty Jo Walker

*<u>Seminole</u>. . . September 12, 1988. . . First Baptist Church. . . Carol Shi, local coordinator
Sponsor: Ladies Activity Day, First Baptist Church

Mona Adkisson	Julia Ewert	Barbara King	Wilma Russell
Nadine Anderson	Linda Fraizer	Shirley Maye	Lois Shoemaker
Nova Dawn Bivens	Jean Frane	Barbara Mendenhall	Lois Small
Cindi Boggs	Pat Garbutt	Ruth Molyan	Polly Stewart
Alix Botsford	Paula Garbutt	Esther Naylor	Lillie Stover
Charles Carter	Jan Garrell	Peggy Neill	Nancy Sullivan
Duba Coates	Mary Glymer	Susan Newberry	Kaylene Thompson
Joy Demer	Susan Hammon	Pat Newell	Sylvia Vance
Pearl Denison	Harriett Howard	Shirley Pfrehem	Bonnie Venil
Bobete Driver	Marie Jarvis	Loretta Reddington	Janett Waddell

*<u>Stillwater</u> . . . September 30, 1987 . . . Payne County Fairground. . . Sue Rose and Thelma Baker, local coordinators
Sponsors: Cimarron Valley Quilters Guild, Pioneer Area Quilters Guild, Patches and Pieces Quilters Guild

Bertha Adams	Iris Fawcett	Dottie Merrill	Vuran Sanders
Cheryl Baker	Jan Fitch	Mary Miller	Fran Sarenson
Sammie Barnard	Betty Gilliam	Sally Murphy	Diana Sargent
Kathy Bolton	Mary Goldsberry	Jackie Neison	Sheila Foxworthy Shannon
Bessie Buntin	Gladys Grant	Mary Lou Paine	Mary Alice Sinton
Phyllis Clark	Mary Groeneman	Juanita Payne	Jane Struthers
Rosalie Drew	Carleen Howell	Helen Marie Ricker	Theresa Sutto
Joyce Eagan	Frances Humphrey	Helen Rogers	Martha Taylor
Marie Ewy	Janet Legere	Helen Rutledge	June Weatherly

*<u>Tulsa</u>. . . April 26, 1988. . . Mabee Center Oral Roberts University . . . Helen Weeks, local coordinator
Sponsor: Green Country Quilters Guild

Jeri Bisel	Gloria Greenlee	Janette Meetze	Cynthia Regone
Dorothy L. Blake	Ruth Guthridge	Ardena Merlock	Birthe Ritsler
Susie Bloss	Glenna Hailey	Brenda Metzinger	Fran Scantlen
Jody Carlson	Mary Harmon	Donna Miller	Sondra Steinberg
Rita Carter	Carol Herman	Lucille Mylar	Laura Thomas
Ann Conti	Bonnie Hontz	Nancy Pfeifer	Alice Thomason
Becky Goldsmith	Murray Lucas	Mary Ramsey	Lu Waas
Deborah Gouchoe	Sharon Masterson	Saloma Ratzlaff	Becky Weeks
Madeline Gray			Barbara Wright

*<u>Woodward</u>. . . November 12, 1987. . . New Horizon United Methodist Church. . . Mary Shank, local coordinator

Lois Arness	Geri Didier	Carol Jenkner	Billy Ann Richards
Sonja Boyd	Syvilla Fields	Edith Johnson	Twyla Rutledge
Billie Brock	Darlene Freerhsen	Evelyn Johnson	Marcella Ruttman
Tootsie Cather	Joy Glass	Rose Marie Leveridge	June Stephens
Madeline Chason	Ethel Graft	Wanda Lynes	Polly Stewart
Jo Anne Chestnut	Ann Hague	Virginia Reger Morton	Elaine Terry
Fern Crispin	Joan Hodges	Lucy Nemecek	Melba Thimling
Teena Dean	Doris Lee Howard	Anita Peck	Laura Thomas
			Linda Williams

INDEX OF QUILTS BY TITLE
(Given by Maker or Owner)

Comprehensive List of Quiltmakers Registered

The Oklahoma Quilt Heritage Project was designed to recognize and affirm the contribution of persons whose quilts were made in or brought to Oklahoma before 1940. Over four thousand quilts were registered across the state, but in many instances, the maker's name was unknown, or the person bringing the quilt was not sure of correct name spelling.

The following list is included in this book for two reasons: to recognize those persons whose quilts were registered, and to refer readers of the book to the research data. The information recorded at the QUILT DAY and a photo of each quilt registered will be placed in the Oklahoma Historical Society archives, Oklahoma City, and it is hoped that persons interested in genealogy, quilts, and regional history will use this material as a basis for research in the future.

---

* Denotes a quiltmaker whose work is pictured in *Oklahoma Heritage Quilts*.

Aaron,	Anna E. Hartle	Arnett,	T.	Baugh,	Rebecca Weldon	Bode,	Maude
	Allen A.	Arnett, OK,	* Four - Mile Quilt Club		Sallie E. Munsey	Boggess,	Artisima
Abel,	Mrs. J. A.	Arnold,	A.J. Benefield (Mrs.)	Baugher,	Zona Frances	Bohgren,	Alma Duckwall
Achter,	Eva		Elizabeth	Baughier,	* Ora Robertson	Bohl,	Mary
Adair,	Edna		Emma	Baughman,	Emma Grace George	Boles,	Edith
Adams,	Beatrice Estelle Landers		Josephine Clemmentine Benfield	Bauman,	Lottie Thompson	Bolinger,	Mrs.
	* Celia Gertrude		Rose Stewart	Baxter,	* Dortha Bourbonnais	Bolt,	Maggie Lillian Alcorn
	Lucinda Watkins	Arnwine,	Joyce Greeawalt	Bay,	Myrtia Chapin	Bond,	Margaret Candace Smith
	Martha	Arpelar, OK,	Quilt Club	Bayless,	Mary Schell	Bonny,	Dorothy Blackmore
	Mary Stewart	Ashby,	Eva Lenora Johnson	Beach,	Rose Loula		John Ann "Annie" Portwood
	Rebecca Padgett	Ashley,	Mrs.	Beall,	Sarah Utterback		Nettie
	Rexie Paine	Ashton,	Eliza Pottinger	Bean,	Leta	Boone,	Della
	* Ruby Jones	Askew,	Mary Elizabeth Talbot	Bearden,	Ora	Bootner,	Estelle Fulcher
Adamson,	Emma Zetta	Athen,	Hallie Lanning		Pauline	Booton,	Lucinda Vaughn
Adcock,	Margaret Maude Flethcher	Atkins,	India Winn	Beattie,	Helen Louise Ledford	Boston,	Evaline Oldham
Adkins,	Mrs. Boyd		Pearl Alexander	Beaver, OK,	Senior Citizens	Boswell,	Nancy
Agra, OK,	Methodist Church Ladies Aid	Atkinson,	Belle	Beck,	Edna L.	Botkin,	Susan Faulk
Ahr Aus,	F. Y.	Auld	Emma D.	Beckeith,	Iva Kinser	Bounds,	Nellie Mae Thomasson
Akard,	Ludie	Austin,	Cynthia Weaver	Bedingfield,	Willie	Bowen,	Alimina Slough
Akers,	Emigene Beak		Emma Bliss Hicks	Beech,	Suzanna Alice Anna	Bower,	Helen Bohgren
Albire,	Harriet Garman	Babb,	Mary Ike	Beeker,	Magdalena	Bowers,	Osa Kimberly
Albright,	Jane		Maude	Begun,	Ada Andrews	Bowler,	Kara Jean
Albrook,	Nattie	Babcock,	Ella May LePage	Belcher,	Nellie Nelson	Bowman,	Annie
Alcorn,	Mollie Savilla Mallett	Baber,	Gertrude Wyatt	Bell,	Agnes Morford		Catherine Nesbitt
Aldridge,	Mrs.	Baden,	Pauline Bussman		Faye Wallace		Rhoda Mae
Alexander,	Alpertenia Julia Owings	Bagley,	Bettie		Marilyn		Rubie E. Wilkerson
Aline, OK,	1st Methodist Church	Bailey,	Minnie Mae Burns		Vivian Barefoot	Boyd,	Etta L. Norman
Allen,	Barbara Straub		Sarah Jane Haymore	Bellamy,	Mrs.		Sam (Mrs.)
	Bell Pope		Y.	Benaon,	Mary Ellen		Sarah Jane Turley
	* Clara Eva Frame	Baker,	Adaline F.	Bender,	Mattie Mae Groat	Boyers,	Ellie Barton
	C. O. (Mrs.)		Adelia Ann Johnson	Benham,	Lucinda Frances Stevens	Bradford,	Laura Green
	Evelyn Frame		Alice	Benneth,	Kari Baukel	Bradshaw,	Ella
	Gladys Maynard		Buena Victoria Trent	Bennett,	Edith		Luanna Risner
	Leota Jackson		Fannie Grafft		Edna		Mrs.
	Lois		Lottie		Epsie Frances Lansess	Branch,	Laura Allen
	Lura Ellen Davis		* "Mollie" Mary Alice	Benson,	Ida Stuart		Matilda Barr
	* Mary Watkins		* Myrtle	Benton,	Jennie Davis	Brandon,	Pearl
	Minnie IvyPearson		Ollie Mae Due	Beree,	Myrtle Swank	Brandt,	Mrs. S.
	Thelma Rogers		Pauline		Sarah E.	Branham,	Clara Tharp
Alley,	Hattie		Rachel Secor	Berg,	Anna Marguerite Neupher	Branscom,	Martha Kendall
Alsup,	Arnie Leath		Ruby Grisso	Bernhardt,	Lucille Garrison	Brashears,	Mrs. R. W.
	Nora Freeman		Ruth Dise	Bernhart,	May Rieff	Bray,	Thula Adila Everett
Altus, OK,	United Methodist Church		Sarah Tash	Bernice, OK,	Baptist Womens Club	Brayfield,	Sarah Kilpatrick
Amdrews,	Misses	Ballard,	* Ciacha Elizabeth Hood	Berrie,	Letha Ann Johnson	Breeding,	* Ethel Smith
Amen,	Lena		Ruby	Berry,	Edith Ticer	Breedlove,	Henryetta
Ammerman,	Allie		Mrs.		Flossie Jenkins	Breeze,	Marcenia Angeline Brown
Amspacher,	Ruby McMahan	Ballou,	Lottie Richards		Juliet Sophia King		Stella Ford
Amstutz,	Esther Moore	Bangs,	Violet Virginia Jordan		Sarah Elen Stine	Brewer,	E. Marie Garrett
Anderson,	Alice Due	Banks,	Fannie	Betts,	Ollie Seabourn		Nora
	Annie Lipscomb	Banta,	Jennie Loue	Bevels,	Clarice Pryor	Brewster,	Addie Winningham
	Cynthia Ann Tyler	Barber,	Angie Fox		Dona		Anna Lee Wilson
	Eliza Jane Yochem	Barefoot,	Carmen		Donie Johnson	Brickman,	Amelia
	Frank		Nancy Clara Withrow		Lillie Mae	Bridgman,	Mrs. Robert S.
	Frieda	Barnard,	Anne Margaret Curry	Bickett,	Fannie R. Marvin	Briggs,	Kathern Owsley
	Laura Sharp		Mrs.	Bickford,	Hazel		Lela McKissack
	* Leona Witcher	Barnes,	Dora Etta	Bigfeather,	Aggie		Mary Hermanski Collier
	* Minnie Frances Witcher		Edith Marie	Biggers,	G.W. (Mrs.)		Radie Beatrice Cain
	Myrtle	Barnett,	* Elizabeth Airington	Biles,	Dorah Belle Pruitt	Brimage,	Lucille
	Paul C. (Mrs.)			Billings, OK,	* Church Group	Brimm,	Claraetta Edwards
	Ruth Boston		Emma Moran	Bills,	Jersline Taylor	Briscoe,	Anna Northington
	Thelma Hughs		Pearl Osburn	Bingham,	Leona Wells		Mary Phelps
Andrews,	* Clara Spangler	Barney,	Ida Mae Tomlinson	Bird,	Ethel F.Carr Schumate	Britton,	Alfa Omega Rois
	Emma Athens	Barnhizen,	Mrs.	Birdwell,	Maxeene Cooper		Burnette Featherstone
	Lillie Ann Swack	Baron,	Sarah Tubbs	Bishop,	Anna Florence Dorland	Brock,	Maude
	* Margarette	Barricklow,	Sarah Ann		Marvin Alice Scott	Brook,	Mary Oliver
	* Martha	Bartlesville, OK,	1st Church of God		Lucy Jones	Brookes,	Claudia Jameaon Phillips
	Mary "Molly" Emma Bain		1st Methodist Church	Bixby, OK,	Methodist Church		Emma Alexandria Garner
	* Rachel	Bartlett,	Dove McConnell	Black,	Annie	Brooksher,	* Margaret Singelton Rose
	Ruth Gibson		Zelmarean Armstrong		Jess	Browder,	Ethel Overall
Anthony,	Ola Christine Click	Basham,	Dixie Mayhew		Locky Jane Burrows	Brown,	Alice
Apache, OK,	Amohalko Club	Baskett,	Minnie		Rose Anna		Artie Anna White
Apple,	Henrietta Harrison	Bass,	Mrs.	Blackwell,	Rowena Angeline		Augustine
	Nellie E. Holder		Nellie	Blaine,	Jewell Zeverly Spann		Edna Jessie Powers
Arapaho, OK,	Baptist Church	Baswell,	Tandy W. (Mrs.)	Blair,	Ella Leonora Hailey Ridenor		Ethel
Arbuckle,	Virginia Maxwell	Bath,	Eliza Rozena Staffen	Blalack,	* Artie Beall Hulsey		Fannie
ArganBright,	Maggie McKee Pollack Bussart	Batt,	Mae	Blanke,	Ricka Bodger		Florence Berry
Armitage,	Josephine	Battle,	Emma	Blanton,	Mary D. Rector		Ina Fay Turner
Armstrong,	Anna Morrison	Baty,	Lillie Marie Meadows	Bloodworth,	Elizabeth Findley		Lavenia Weed
	Edith Smith	Baugh,	Ethel Ricketts	Boatright,	Catherine Wilson		Lillie Schulz
	Margaret Ward		Naomi Schmalhorst	Bobeck,	Pauline Kubik		Lou Lois Berry

Brown,	Lucy Pettit
	* Martha Mills
	Mary M.
	Mattie Ellen Smith
	Mavie Olene Lee
	Myrtle Lydia
	Ola
	Polly Roxie Akin
	Tennessee Walker Winfield
	Vivian Eileen Christian
Browning,	Lola Frances Speir Phillips
Bruce,	Lena Mills
	* Nannie Samuel
Brunson,	Pet England
Bryan,	Ruth
Bryant,	Alice
	* Florence Shinn
	Maxine W.
	Moe
	Nellie Dudley
	Nellie Burr
	Nola Stricklin
Buchanan,	Bonnie Bell Butler
Bucklew,	Lois Mackey
	Pearl
Buckminster,	Alice
	Alice Finkenbinder
	Minnie Horn
Bud,	Sallie
Bullen,	Mrs. J. T.
Bunn,	Juanita Babb
Buntzel,	Mary F.
Burch,	Myrtle
	Lillie Carroll
Burcham,	Pearl
Burditt,	Ellen Rogers
	Mertle Rogers
Burgess,	Eliza Evans
	Josephine S.
	Lorna Mae Earlywine
	Sarah Benham
Burkhart,	Sophia Bergman
Burleson,	Alice Violet
	Eliza Adine Russum
Burneyville, OK,	Quilters
Burr,	Emma Sarah Mabry
Burris,	Georgia Evelyne Youngblood
	Gillie
Burrus,	Addie Davis
Burton,	Clara Caroline Miller
	Milanda Catner
Busby,	Mary Emily Thomason
	Mary Hadassah Battenfield
Bush,	Isabell
Bussey,	Cora
	Gladys
Butcher,	Laura Wasson
Butler,	Ada Harper
	Ella Luella Stanberry
	Emily Frances Baker
	Mabel
	Mabel Bell
	Marie Black
	Nora Fincannon
	Ollie
	Stella Johnson
Buts,	Arepha Wallace
Buttler,	Marie Black
Buttman,	Maggie Mae Emmack
Button,	Vinnie Watts
Byers,	Annie Noe
	Lottie
Byram,	* Lola White
	Ozella Lee
Byrd,	Mary Etta Jolly
Byrum,	Elsie
Cabe,	* Sallie Seay
Cabiness, OK,	Quilt Club
Caddell,	Katie
Cahill,	Mary Diamond
Caldwell,	Maryora Randles
Callaway,	Sarah Bell Phillips
Calvert,	Pearl Dorsett
Camargo, OK,	* Assembly of God Church
Cammerer,	Sophia Westrup
Campbell,	Ethel Brady
	Eva Lea Cummings
	Florence
	Harry (Mrs.)
	Norma
	Pearl
Canadian, OK,	Methodist Church
Canfield,	Mrs. G. W.
Cannon,	Catherine Taylor
Canute, OK,	Christian Science Mission Society
	Community Church
Capehart,	Betty Ann Lewis
Caperton,	Edith Lee George
	Ruby Hackler
Capshaw,	Nancy Hogan
Carce,	Mary Margurete
Cardin,	Mrs. J. L.
Cardwell,	Odie Ethel Tunnell Wells
Carlisle,	Augusta Hoelsher
Carlsile,	Bettie Bennett
Carmack,	Erma Burleson
Carpenter,	Eunice Goodbary
	Grace Roberts
	Liz
	Mary Ann Thompson
	Susan Batdorf
Carrier,	Mary Lind Faulkner
Carrier, OK,	Congregational Church
Carris,	Jennie McNurlen
Carrol,	Rebecca Stice Hart Hughes
Carroll,	Lela Myra Stewart
Carruth,	Susan
Carson,	Blanche Harris
Carter,	Sallie Jane Brandon
	* Serena Josephine Guy
Case,	Lois Crispin
Casey,	Mae
Casper,	Ellen Riddle
Cate,	Frances Bowman
Cather,	Leva
Cavett,	Sarah Josephine
Cayton,	Blanche Wall
Cement, OK,	Christian Home
Center,	Ruby Nelson
Chadwick,	* Gertrude Butler
Chaffin,	Leona
	Carol
Chamberlin,	Laura
Chambers,	Jayme Ledgerwood
	Sarah Mikesel
Chance,	Julia Coffelt
Chaney,	Sarah McCall
Chapman,	Lida Songer
	* Lucinda Hepsibal
Chappel,	Fannie Durbin
Charlson,	Tahlie
Chartier,	Mabel Rounds
Chelsea, OK,	Baptist Church
	Extension Club
Cheney,	Frana Owens
Chenoweth,	* Cora King
	* Mary McElwain
	* Mildred Livengood
	* Nancy Elizabeth Palmer
	* Rosanna King
Cherokee, OK,	Jolly Neighbor Club
	Enid Senior Citizens
Cherry,	Bettie L. Gillmore
	Ella Nora Markwell
Chester,	Ozara
Childress,	Mrs.
Chism,	Lizzie T. Wells
Chitwood,	Lela Iris Hiatt
Christian,	Margaret Kelsay Conner
	Mary Phyle
Clagg,	Dollie Lavina Watta
Claremore,	Methodist Church
Clark,	Alice Kirby Eyler
	Bertha Hardestry
	Emma
	Lavenia
	Mahalea
	Martha Ann
	* Mary Elizabeth Ittner
Clasen,	Alice M. Nieuwenhuis
	Dorothy O.
Classen,	Mrs. John
Claus,	Cindy
Clem,	Verna Lucas
Clements,	Gertrude May Thomas
Cleveland,	Ernie Bell Belshe
	Lousia Jane Tucker Matthews
Cleveland, OK,	1st Christian Church
	1st Methodist Church
	Presbyterian Church
Clinton,	Ella
Clinton, OK,	* Chalitso Club
	Christian Church
Cloud,	Elba Jane Hughes
	Sarah Steele Cloud
Cobb,	Ethel
	Lou Emma Prewett
Cobbs,	Avis
Cochran,	* Almeda
	Daisy Estelle Ward
	Maude Green
Coen,	Millie Bailey
Coffey,	Lou Ellen Simcox
	Lou Mina Jane Clark
	Mabel Miller
Coffman,	Alice Katherine Hendrix
Cogar, OK,	Extention Homemakers
Coil,	Pearl Amstutz
Colbert,	Athenius Folsum
Colbert , OK,	Methodist Church
Cole,	Esther
	Mrs.
	Susannah Serena Jones
Coleman,	* Etta Mouser
	Minnie Alice Stowe
	Polly
Collier,	Opal
Collins,	J. A. (Mrs.)
	Rosetta Canaday
Collinsworth,	Ethel McBride
Combs,	Dovey
Coney,	Omie Oea Williams
Conner,	Mattie
Cook,	Bernice Johnson
	Martha Busbee
	Minerva Catherine Daugherty
	Nettie
	Nettie Widner
	Sara Elizabeth Mullins Heidelberg
Cooksey,	Mary Belle Bredlove
Coon,	Jane
	Mrs.
Cooper,	Ada L.
	Elizabeth Ann Eyster
	Myrtle Kelley Grandall
Copan, OK,	Quilting Club
Cope,	Bertha
Copher,	Ida Tucker
Corbin,	Annie B. Caldwell
Cordell,	Dannile
Cordes,	* Margaretha
Corley,	Mollie
Cornell,	Lavinia Wilhide
	Valeria Eddress Faulkerson
Coulson,	Mrs. J. W.
Courtney,	Mrs.
Cox,	Belle Langley
	Clara
	Mona Gray
Coykendall,	Edith Turner
Crabb,	Mattie Maude Burnham
Craft,	Elizabeth Jane
Crafton,	Mary
	Mary Catherine Leoser
Craig,	Emma Hicks
	Genevia Stovall
	* Mary Emline Casey
Craighead,	Erma
Crain,	Ada Porter
Cranford,	Lethey Ann Lambeth
Craven,	Nancy Elizabeth Brookshire
Crawford,	* Elizabeth
	Elizabeth Muirheid
	Helen Gibson
	Mary Elizabeth Gash
	Nettie E. Nelson
Creachaum,	Rebecca Hyne
Creason,	Ida Klopfenstein
Creech,	Fannie Louisia McCrea
	Mae
	Nancy Mae Keys
Crispin,	Blanch Elder
Criss,	Grace L. Robinson
Crittenden,	Becky
Crizan,	Mammie Montgomery
Crocker,	Mattie Johanna Belcher
	Nellie Grey
	Sara Melinda Rich
Crockrell,	Belle Fink
Crosby,	* Mary Ann McCann
Cross,	* Ona Wagoner
Crouch,	Amy Garrett
	Grace Elizabeth Platt
Crow,	Luna Fugate
Crowder,	Rose Ann
Crowley,	Markie
Croxton,	Ina Cuthbertson
Crusha,	* Elzora Mae Lyon
Cruzan,	Clarah C.
Culbertson,	Linnie
Cullen,	Naomi Pace
Cullers,	Anna
Culver,	Marcella
Cummins,	* Katie B. Long
Cummings,	James
Cunningham,	Carrie Snow
	Delilah
	Margaret Ann Cottrell
	Nellie
	Sandy
Curtis,	* Alta Alma Gass
	Lola Boling
Cushman,	* May E. Pringle
Cyril, OK,	Rebecca Lodge
Dacus,	Lucille Johnson
Dail,	Rose Evelyn White
Dailey,	Betty
Dalgarn,	Mary Hayner
Damon,	Mabel Diercks
Daniel,	Lillian Ruth Daniels
	Ida Matilda Steinberg
	Lois Gifford
Daniels,	Rebecca Jane Banks
Dansby,	Ila
Carby,	Bessie Kerns
Daugherty,	Beaulah
	Katherine Ramey
	Maude
	Pearl Barefoot
Davenport,	Zora
Davenport, OK,	Good Neighbor Club
Davidson,	Elizabeth Motley
	Elsie Conner
	Laura Montgomery
Davie,	Gertie
Davis,	Addie Theodosia Crites
	Ann
	Eleanor Hauck
	Emma Jernigan
	Fannie Evelyn Morey
	Ida Mae
	Lola
	Lola Bishop
	Lucy Thompson
	* Margaret Brown
	Martha Ellen Coffman
	Martha Jane Coffman
	Minnie Mae Long
	Myrtle Staughn
	Nancy McGarity
	Sarah O.
Davison,	Roma Ann Hiatt
Day,	Zelma Batt
Deal,	Elizabeth Clements
Dean,	Ada Pickens
	Madaline McAllister
	Sallie Anderson
	Virginia
Deaton,	Sindy Swift
Deckinson,	Nannie Estell
Deer,	Elina Harris
Deere,	Donna
DeFratus,	Dessie Lee Blackburn
Dellsaver,	Marie
Deneson,	Theda
Denham,	Gertrude
Dennett,	Delpha Pfister
Deo,	Ada
Deom,	Mary Antionette Belva
Desilver,	Edith Allen
Desmond,	Hattie Egnor
Deulen,	Lettie P. Vlmer
Deveney,	Mollie
Dever,	Martha Jane Richardson Austin
Dewey, OK,	1st Christian Church
DeWit,	Sarah
Dickens,	Minnie Amoretta Parkins
Dickerson,	Anna V. Hanes
Dickey,	Fannie
	Mary
	Mary Elizabeth Daugherty
Dickson,	Addie
	Mina
Diercks,	Flossie
Diffendaffer,	Creta
Diffie,	Daisey Whitt
Diggs,	Mary
Dilday,	Visie Ann Petty
Dill City, OK,	Methodist Church
Dillard,	Gladys Pursley
Diller,	Callie Kite
Dilley,	Lucinda
Dillon,	Anna Agnes
	Sandy Grider
Dinwiddie,	Ella
Dixon,	* Gerald
	* Mary Otis
	* Ouida Wilder
	* Rosa
	Rosa Jane Smith
Dobbs,	Bessie
	Creta
	Katherine Lewis
Dobozy,	Bimmie Rosebud
Dobson,	Alpha Belle Harrington
Docherty,	Cledith Marie Harrington
Donar,	* Mary Phipott
Donley,	Beulah Mae Love
	Ella B. Louthan
Dorser,	Florence Stamper Glenn
Dorsey,	Mrs.
Drain,	Lula Beebee
Drake,	Esther Aletta Williams
	Myra
Dryden,	Lorene
Dubbens,	Martha
Dudek,	Mytle McKinney Burcham
Dudley,	Maude Smith
Duey,	Emma Houston
Duke, OK,	Community Club
Dulabahm,	Gertrude
Duncan,	Edith
	Eva
	John H. Jr.
	Margaret Smallwood
Dunfee,	Mrs. T. W.
Dunn,	Alice Baker Nickles
	Ida
	Maybelle Grace Ozmun
Dyhes,	Mary Ann
Eagles,	Dellar June Sexton
Eakins,	Mrs. Albert E.

Eargle,	Ida Fuller
Earnest,	Leota Castar
Eastwood,	* Mrs.
Easter,	Mrs. R. A.
Easterly,	Ophelia Montgomery Taylor
	Ruth
Eastes,	Kitty
Eaton,	Molly Frances Alberty
Ebbs,	Mrs. R. E.
Eddings,	* Caroline Criner
Eden,	Meg
Edison,	Hat Holder
Edmond, OK,	American War Mothers
Edwards,	Elia C. Embry
	Elizabeth
	* Elsie Smith
	Verla Adams
Eeed,	Veda Olson
Eggleston,	Mrs. O. H. Waite
El Reno OK,	Mt. Zion Church
Eldelm,	Leah Audersau
Elder,	Annie
	Mabel Nowaka
Eldridge,	Fay Winn
Elk City, OK,	Merritt Quilting Club
Ellerman,	Mittie
Elliff,	Joy Betts
Elliott,	Mary Elizabeth Wooten
Ellis,	Florence V. Smith
	Mamie
	Mrs.
Ellison,	Inez
	Ruby Hustand
Ellsworth,	Jo Ella Smith
Elrod,	* Rohesa Anne Harmon
Elrode,	* Gladys Lawrence
Elwood,	Sarah Josephine
Emert,	Ruby Adair
Emmack,	Delaney Ann
Endress,	Rachel Hager
Engelbert,	Lulu Paula
England,	Utevia
English,	Hattie Rose McKnight
Enid, OK,	Central Christian Church
	Congregational Church
	Mennonite Brethren Church
	Sunnyside Extension Homemakers
Epperson,	Hazel Betts
	Mrs.
Eppler,	Bessie Violet Scruggs
Essary,	Florence Ray
Estelle,	* Arminda Lucinda Cooper
Ethington,	Eva
	Margaret
Eutsler,	Ethel May Bertenshaw
Evans,	Dollie Littlejon MIller
	N. Rose
	Nannie Eyler Sill
	Nellie Jane Key
Everett,	Mary Annie White
	Mettie Williams
Ewing,	Effie Lindley
	Elizabeth Petters
Ewy,	Lizzie
Eye,	Adelaide
	Anna Kaffman
Eyler,	Katherine Emerick
Fair,	Mary Elizabeth Hooper
Fairview, OK,	Quilt Club
Fambrough,	Sue Peterson
Fancher,	Margaret Gilliand
Fant,	Laura Blanke
Fargo, OK.	Church Guild
Faris,	Maggie Elizabeth Lewis
Farnsworth,	Sarah Howe
Farrell,	Henrietta L. Clasen
Farrer,	Sallie Oliverb
Farris,	Ollie Geneva Heard
Faulkerson,	Mamie Cook
Faulkner,	Bettie Beatrice Brown
	Ida Caroline Buford
	Jen McClellan Foreman
	* Pernety Arno Billings
Faust,	Jewel Roberts
Feeback,	Hattie
Fees,	Marie Ausmus
Fenn,	Joanna Mae Dwelle
Ferguson,	Marie Coleman
Ferree,	Blake
	Mary Ellen Calico
Fess,	Ina Hunt
Feuquay,	Beatrice Adams
Fields,	Cora Bell Bess
	Maggie
Fike	Mrs. Douglas
Findlar,	Agnar
Finkenbinder,	Mrs. Charles
Finnel,	Constance
Fischer,	Anna Schoebachler
Fisher,	Florence Barricklow
Fitzgerald,	Mrs. Marshall
Fitzpatrick,	Clara King
Flanagan,	Clara

Fletcher,	Hazel Love
Fletcher, OK,	Christian Home
Flinn,	Zella Ashenhurst
Floyd,	Carol Rambo
	* Dorothy
	Jessie Turner
	Mattie Gallaher
	Mrs.
Focht,	Addie
	Minnie Withers
Folsom,	Blanche
Foquata,	Nannie
Forbis,	Irene McWhorter
Foreaker,	Sara Ann Karl
Foreman,	Fannie Broiles
Formen,	Helen Busboom
Forrest,	Mary Ella Cox
Forrester,	Mrs.
Forter,	Blanche Brink
	Matilda
Fortney,	Ruth Kelter
Foster,	Agnes
	* Dorothy
	Edna Brown
	Joyce
	* Margaret
	Mary Harris
	Mattie
	Myranda Elizabeth
	Nina Smith
Foulk,	* Maggie Clark
Fouty,	Mary Ellen
Fowler,	Leona Phelps Allen
	Lucille
	Mary Ellen
Foyil, OK.	Methodist Church
Frame	Geraldine Coleman
Frank,	Kate
	* Lillie Mae Graumann
Franks,	Magdelina Harris
	Marion Elizabeth Brock
Frazier,	Sally
Freeman,	* Cordelia Jones
	Emmy Baker Powell
	* Zula Mings
Freese,	Clementine Kolb
Frey,	Elizabeth McCool
	Millie Reed
Fricke,	* Marie Magdene
Friesen,	Susie M. Wiens
Fritchman,	Elizabeth
Fritsch,	Rebbeca McKerr
Fritz,	Mrs.
Frost,	Emma
	Kate
Fry,	Ida Bell
	Ida Rickett
Ft. Worth, Texas,	Grace Bible Church
Fudge,	Mrs. Daniel
Fugate,	Rebecca Anna Lura Abercrombie
Fuller,	Willie Fortune
	* "Sis"
Fullerton,	Jimmie Law Bevers
Fulton,	Mattie Russell Brister
Fussel,	Violet Stoll
Gaither,	Lou Parker McClellan
Galloway,	* Nancy M.
Ganes,	Emily Snow
Garber, OK,	New Bethany Church
Gard,	Mrs. Jon
Garden City, KS,	Presbyterian Ladies Aid
Gardner,	Gladys
	Hattie
Garnhart,	* Anna Catherine Hummel Markey
Garrerr,	Ethel Mae
	Nola Mae Davis
Garrison,	Bessie
	Lola Price
	Pearl
Gary,	Van-noy
Gaskill,	Carrie Perry
Gastineau,	Mrs. James R.
Gates,	Amanda Cracken
	Floy Perkins
	Peter
Gatewood,	Florence
Garliff,	Ella Frances Henry
Gaylor,	Gladys
Geary, OK,	* Methodist Church
Geiger,	Elva
Gentis,	Sara
Gentis, AR,	Assembly of God Church
George,	Anna Mae Nolin
	Della Campbell
	Margaret "Maggie" Green
	Mary Boyington
	Mrs.
Germab,	Eva S.
Gholson,	* Tabitha Morton
Gibbs,	Cordellia Sims
	Mary Cecil
Gibson,	Bele Clayton
	Cleo Fitzgerald Hobbs

Gibson,	Emily
	Lena
	Mattie Denton
	Nan
	Sarah Johnson
	Viola Elwood
Gigoux,	Alma
	* Minnie Fish
	Viola Ester
Gilbert,	Carolina A.
	Fannie
	Vivian Scott
Gillette,	Emma Louise Wilde
Gilmore,	Echo Elizabeth Porter
Giroux,	Geneva Wright
Glasgow,	Alice
Glass,	Myrtle Lucille Horne
Gleason,	* Susie Minnie
Gleaves,	Alice Perrine
Glenn,	Cora Rankin
Godsell,	Dora
Gohmert,	Johanna Fechner
Gold,	Pamelia Jane Teeters
Goldsboro,	Maggie
	Pauline
Goodman,	Flo Pringle
	Mary E. Brown
Goodner,	* Verlinda Stanridge
Gookin,	Mrs. Virgil
Gordon,	Emma Wolf
Gore,	* Sidney Sophia Cather
Gorman,	Fannie R.
Gorton,	Artie
Gould,	Anna Arvilla Robinson
Gowey,	Mary Howard
Graft,	Ethel Jones
	Nolous Carmichael
Graham,	Alberta Anderson
	Mildred Smith
	Sarah Bryant
	Sarah Joyner
	Viola
Grammill,	Allie Smith
	Maedene
Grandon,	Ellen
Grandstaff,	Janet Reich
Granes,	EMS
	Mary Ellen
Granite, OK,	* 1st Baptist Church
Grant,	Ella
	Minnie
Grant, OK,	School Students 1932
Graper,	Jewell
Graumann,	Erra
Gray,	Mrs. Franklin
Gray,	Dempsey Bussey
	Martha Ellen Daugherty
Greaves,	Mary Stewart
Greeley Co.	Church of the Savior
Green,	Birdie Dee Clark
	E. B. (Mrs.)
	Golda
	Hazel
	* Mattie James
Greenhaw,	Rosa Bell
Greenlee,	Lillian Hobbs
Greenwood,	Dora J. Gilpatrick
Greer,	Mrs.
	Rachel Harmon
Greeson,	Freddie Lee Standfier
Gregory,	Esther
	Fannie
	Susan
	Velma Nichols
Gribble,	Bertie Lucil Briggs
Grider,	Nancy Jane Summers
Griebel,	* Florence Nonnamaker
Grieshemer,	Grace
Griffin,	Lillie Pence
	Ethna
Grigsby,	Estelle
Grisso,	Sarah Addie Smith
Grizzelle,	Myrtle Leanna Lee
Grossett,	Clara Miller Price
Grove,	Catherine Vanderford
	Lillie
Grove, OK,	1st Baptist Church
Grundy,	Ruth
Guffey,	Eva L. Lindsey
	Mary Elizabeth Poindexter
	Sarah E. Lewis
Guinn,	Susan L.
	Maxie Pryor
Gunn,	Lucy Ellen Brown
Guthridge,	Anna
Guthrie,	Eugenia
Guy,	Dora Lee Dotson
Guymon, OK.	Christian Church
	Eula Community
Haas,	Gilbert G.
Hackett,	Annalee
	Mary Ellen Bowen
Hackler,	Ada Hill

Hager,	Lucretia Show
Haggard,	Bertha L. Palmer
Haileyville, OK,	Christian Church
Haines,	Betty Jo
	Emma
	Mrs.
Hair,	Lula
Hale,	Annie Lee Cassell
	Caroline Frances Price
	Sara Syrena Lee
Haley,	Pauline Branigen
Hall,	Alice E.
	Margy S.
	Martha Smith
	Mary
	Mrs. Noah
Halloway,	Neva Olsen
Hamburger,	Katie Harrouff
Hamilton,	Colleen Lindle
	* Daisy
	Delphia P.
	Elizabeth
	Laura
	Martha
	Hammer, Mary
Hammond,	Margaret
	Margaret Lydia
	Nancy Catherine Creps
	Sarah Adaline Hatfield
Hammons,	Martha Elizabeth
Hampel,	Julia Wenzl
Hampton,	Clydie Kitty
Hancock,	* Elizabeth Ellen Washburn
	Sybil Blanche Sanford
	Vivian Whitman
Handy,	Mary
Hanes,	Anna Katheryn Eyel
	Delia Thornton
	Ina
Hanley,	Mable
	Mrs. R. E.
Hanna,	* Elzaradz Quradice
	* Nancy Martin
Hanson,	Mary Fuller
Hardestry,	Jeannie Stennett
Hardesty, OK,	Quilting Club
Hardin,	Laura Powell
	Ruby Briggs
Haries,	Margaret Lee
Harlow,	Mrs.
	Sarah Elizabeth Renfrow
Harmon,	Mrs.
	Mattie Walker
Harnden,	Leona Mae Craig
Harney,	Elizabeth
Harp,	Mrs.
Harper,	Mrs.
	Viola L.
Harris,	Autumn
	Bertha Dale
	Callie Smith
	Margaret
	Margaret Ann Myer
	Sarah Elizabeth
	Theora Greer
	Tillie Hearne
Harrison,	Ida Jane Wix
	Catherine Dimler
Harroun,	Anna Anderson
Hart,	Bertha Zinng
	Evelyn N.
	Mary E. Smith
Hartford, AR,	West Harmony Baptist Church
Hartle,	Maude Boyer
Hartzler,	Elizabeth Bontrager
Harvey,	Eliza Ann Polley
Harwell,	Emma Dale
Hatfield,	Kate Pauls
Haverstick,	Hawkins
Hawad,	Mary
Hawkins,	Flora Byrd
	Martha
	Mattie
	Maude
Hawks,	Elva S. Parks
	* Rosina Bader
Haworth,	Harriet Baker
Haws,	Emily Mae Shotwell
	* Hershel Harold
Hawthorne,	Hazel Irene Carr
Haxel,	Della Iola Ketner
Hay,	Verda Ellen Hayward
Hayes,	Esther Addie James
Hayner,	Myrtle
	Mrs.
Haynes,	Jean
	Nancy Josephine Johnson
Hays,	Gertrude Pierce
	Margaret
Hayward,	Laura Isabelle
Heard,	Mary Alice
Hearrd,	Violet Mary
Hearth,	Laura Elizabeth

Hearth,	Mary Belle	
Heartsill,	Margaret "Maggie" E. Bond	
Heath,	Leota C. Sharrock	
Heavner,	Clara Dean M.	
Hebden,	Adelia Danks	
Hedke,	Sybil Smith	
Hedrick,	Nidrah Edwards	
Hefley,	Mary	
	Minnie Rose Gould	
Heflin,	Agnes	
Heim,	Lealor	
Heisler,	Mrs.	
Helm,	Ota Click	
Helterbran,	Lola Christy	
Helton,	Lucy Aken	
Henderson,	Bertha Ellen Hook	
Hendley,	Eureda	
Hendricks,	* Ruth Naomi	
Henke,	Amber A.	
	Minnie Kase	
Henrichs,	Elsie Belfeldt	
Henry,	Flora	
	Mary Groff Miller	
Henserson,	Coras	
Hensley,	Addie Wheeler	
	Mary Emily Mullen	
Herald,	Bessie	
	Katie	
Herbert,	Esther P.	
	Hanna Summer	
Hermanski,	Emma Fancher	
Herren,	Edgar	
	Val Ford	
Herrin,	Ada Dell Hayes	
Herron,	Olive Gertude Leseney	
Hervey,	Merle	
	Mrs.	
Herzberg,	Mrs. Levi	
Hickman,	Margaret Hanson	
Hicks,	Alma	
	Jewel	
	Mary Edith Tarbet	
Hiebert,	Selma Erona	
Higdon,	Bernice Gates	
Higgins,	Inez Rebecca Hooper	
	Minnie Olson	
Hightower,	Amy Vaughn Allen	
	Mary Elizabeth "Molly" Davidson	
Hill,	Amanda Crocker	
	Emma Hamilton Clark	
	Nell Reeves	
Hiner,	Icalone Agnes Malsbury	
	Mary Evelyn Harris	
Hines,	Mrs. Jim	
Hinkle,	Christine Dilday	
Hix,	Betty	
Hixson,	Mary Temperance Rice	
Hobbs,	Annie Rainey	
	Pearl Jay	
Hockman,	Genevie Carley	
Hodges,	Maggie Campbell	
Hoeffer,	Freida Brokop	
Hoffman,	Detrick P.	
	Lena Brown	
Hogan,	Sarah Terry	
Holaday,	Mary Agnes Walker	
Holbrook,	Lucy Jane Walden	
	Myrinda Ann	
	Rachael Carter	
Holcomb,	Lela McManus	
Holder,	Agnes Bush	
Holinger,	Maggie	
Holland,	Garnet Clark	
	Johnnie Chilcoat	
	Maxine Bolen	
Hollar,	Lura Pierce	
Holley,	Majorie Leecraft	
	Mary Ellen Griggs	
Holloway,	Laura Irene Wegant	
Holman,	Cora Difendaffer	
Holmes,	Cecil C. Wheeler	
Holmstrom,	Mrs. V. A.	
Holt,	* Nettie Wiedenkofer	
Holway,	Helen Freeman	
Holzrichter,	Lena	
Hoobler,	Essie	
Hook,	Bertha Ellen	
Hooner,	Gladys	
	Mrs.	
Hooper,	Inez Rebecca Higgins	
	Mary Emily Owen	
Horn,	Nan	
Horner,	Mary Ellen	
Horning,	Barbara	
Horton,	Laura Featherston	
Hostetter,	* Allie Mae Wallace	
Hough,	Nedda	
House,	Annie	
	Mary Petete	
Houston,	Luna	
Howard,	Laura Baker	
Howell,	"Mollie" Mary Ethel Madding	
	Myrtle Lampkins	
Howland,	Lucy Baker	
Hubert, OK,	Swimmer Baptist Church	
Huckaby,	Sarah Fisher	
Huddle,	Mrs.	
Huddleston,	Mable Blair	
	Ethel Pendleton	
Hudiburg,	Annie (Nancy Ann) Gray	
Hueskoetter,	* Marie Magdene Fricke	
Huff,	Cleo Bennett	
	Josephine Martin	
	Sara E.	
Huffman,	Irris Smith	
	Ann	
Hughes,	Cassie Precure	
	Emma	
	Mamie Bexla Howell	
Hughs,	Molly	
Huline,	Lily Moore	
Hulsey,	Sarah C. Beall	
Hulston,	Lela Robison	
Human,	Mattie Russell	
Humbard,	Mary M. Cook	
Hummel,	Lois A.	
Hummell,	Ella Mae Carpenter	
Humphrey,	Ethel Alvina Berg	
Humphries,	Mary Elizabeth Barlow	
Hunricks,	Mary Suduman	
Hunt,	Anna Belle Chowning	
	Jessie,	
	Lloyd Landrum	
	Sallie J. Hyatt	
Hunter,	Larissa Tyler Eaton	
	Mary Magdalene "Dolly" Henry	
Hunter, OK,	Methodist Church	
Hurt,	Hanna Alice Marsh Kachel	
Huskey,	Ellen Mae Vincent	
	Ruby LaRue Key	
Hutchinson,	Alma	
	Mrs.	
	Sarah Jane Tweedy	
Hutton,	Susan House	
Ibach,	Marie	
Idayes,	Era Anna	
Indiahoma, OK,	Quilt Club	
Ingersoll, OK,	Christian Church	
Ingram,	Delphine Beach	
Inman,	Valda	
Ireland,	Genezia law	
Isaacs,	Myrtle Bell Andrews	
Isbell,	Mary Watson	
Isch,	Beulah	
	Clyde	
Isenberg,	Edna Minnehouse	
Israel,	* Maria Gregg	
Ittner,	Mary Lucy Coleman	
Ivey,	Willa May	
Jackson,	* Belle Zona Thompson	
	Maggie Creech	
	Mary	
	Mary Owens	
	Ramona Jean Chasteen	
James,	Callie Renfro	
	* Mattie O. Green	
	Mrs.	
Jameson,	Rosa Doll	
Jamison,	Lounettie Merrell	
	Mildred Moore	
Janes,	Mary Belle Turney	
Jarvis,	Pearl	
Jeffries,	Lena Vance	
Jenicek,	Mary Stehno	
Jenkins,	Edner Gertrude Gassaway	
	* Elizabeth Jane Wray	
	Frances M.	
	Margaret Davis	
Jenks, OK,	1st Baptist Church	
	1st Christian Church	
Jennings,	Clara Maude White	
	Eliza Wheeler	
	Mary E.	
	Mollie Stutts	
Jernigan,	Emma Field	
	Pauline Klutts	
Jerome,	Carrie	
	Ida Mae Trumbo	
Jinkins,	* Elizabeth Jane Wray	
John,	* Ann Evans	
	Bessie	
	Elizabeth McKnight	
Johns,	Katie Stutzman	
Johnson,	Arizona Addline Davis	
	Dorthea Ada	
	Elizabeth Blodgett	
	Florence May Stiles	
	Johnnie Lucille McBride	
	Leona Margaret	
	Letha Long King	
	* Lizzie Burch Palmer	
	Louis H.	
	Martha Jones	
	Mary Elizabeth Pulliam	
	Minnie Benefield	
	Mrs. Jo Neal	
Johnson,	Olive L. Nicholls	
	Opal Weeks	
Johnston,	Nell	
Jones,	Anna	
	Belle Able	
	Catherine	
	Elizabeth	
	Elizabeth Serrepti Campbell	
	Elizabeth Tender	
	Freda Coshen	
	* Gladys Rush	
	Helen Marie	
	Irene Mershon	
	Jane Price	
	Libby Cole	
	Lillie Woodard	
	Mabel	
	Martha Allred	
	Margaret Elizabeth Lindsey	
	Myrtle Lanning	
	Nellie Belle Detherge	
	Nora Boyd	
	Rella	
	Ruth Menasco	
Jordan,	Lena C.	
Joyner,	Martha	
Julian,	Della Hill	
	Laura Ellen Baum	
	Nora B. Cox	
Kachel,	Mary Maggie Bukowski	
Kaiser,	Lydia Boepple	
Kamphaus,	* Dorothy Winkler	
	Frances Mann	
Kangley,	Mrs.	
Karber,	Luella Wiens	
Kasterke,	Mary Louise	
Kay,	Doroth Clemintine Ash	
.	* Eliza	
Kaye,	Elizabeth Francis Langford	
Kearnes,	Nancy Ellen Reese	
Keegan,	Margaret Irene	
Keener,	Annie	
Keesee,	Ruby	
Kehemund,	Minnie Ehlers	
Keith,	Clara Coleman	
Kellar,	Minerva Jane	
Keller,	Minnie M. Teal	
	Vernie Ragsdale	
Kelley,	Annie	
	* Clella Harris	
	Dorcas	
	Florence	
	Jeannie Louise Meyer	
Kelly,	Juna	
	Lydia McKinzie	
	Susan	
Kelso,	* Sarah Glezen	
Keltner,	Ida Conner	
Kemmerer,	Maggie	
Kempka,	Teafilia "Theo" Bieberdorf	
Kendall,	M. Clara Wilson	
Kennedy,	Beatrice Fulton	
	Lillian Gilmore	
	Theo Anthony	
Kenney,	Viola Logan King	
	Julia Lemastus	
Kennicutt,	Julia Ann Coffman	
Kenton,	Martha Jay Heavner	
Keota, OK,	Ladies' Circle	
Kerne,	Malinda Bedaine	
Kerr,	Mamie Worthy	
Kesler,	Ethel Hardin	
Ketterman,	Margaret Davis	
Keys,	Mary McDaniel	
Kibbe,	Nancy Smith	
Kilcrease,	Adelia Griswald	
Kilgore,	Elizabeth Rosengrant	
Killingsworth,	Ina Jones	
	Mary Etta Spurr	
Kilpatrick,	Molly	
Kindley,	Grace Mae Jackson	
Kindred,	Sara Lou Summers	
King,	Alice Lewis	
	Arizona	
	Estella P. Hixson Reese	
	Isibell	
	Jo Ann Keller	
	Joan	
	Josie	
	Little Maude Whisenant	
	* Luticia Reeves Fancher	
	Nora Whisenant	
	Sarah Elizabeth Slack	
	U. (Mrs.)	
Kinman,	Ina Mildred Hunt	
Kinney,	Beulah Mae Timberlane	
	Grace M.	
Kiowa, OK,	Gaither Community Sewing Club	
Kipps,	Hanna Rice	
Kirch,	Emma Miller	
Kirchmeier,	Nellie Ann Courtney	
Kirk,	Alma Butler	
Kirkwood,	Erma Blount	
Kirmse,	* Martha Cordes	
Kittell,	Carrie Parrish	
Kizziar,	Mrs. R. B.	
Klaassen,	Edna Bushman	
Klingsick,	Alice	
Knepper,	Mrs.	
Knight,	* Cora Lee Riley	
	Della Ann Main	
	May	
Knowles,	Annie	
	Mary Jane Allen	
Knox,	Bessie Fenwick	
	Lela Virginia Fritts	
Koch,	Abby	
	Bessie	
Koeppen,	Ola Shipman	
Koger,	Monna Calvert	
Konawa, OK,	Methodist Missionary Society	
Kravitzky,	Hanna Morrison	
Kriel,	Margaret Ann Schaeffer	
Krone,	Jamima Lay	
Krueger,	Ella Kirmse	
Kyle,	May Tanner	
	Pearl Robinson	
Kyler,	* Judith Hbuer	
La Rue,	Nellie Myrtle Kizer	
Labude,	Mary Dunfee	
Lackey,	Eva Brown	
Lacy,	Ida Belle Farr	
Lading,	Julia Meyers	
Lady,	Sadie Siegenthaler	
Lamar,	Mrs.	
	* Natolia Maree Shaffer	
Lamb,	Iva Mae	
Lambert,	Frances Helen Stephenson	
Lamm,	Doris	
	Mary	
Lamson,	Alice	
Lane,	Belle Mooney	
Langford,	Bill	
	Edie	
	Julie	
Langley,	Ruth Ann	
Lankford,	Katie Sparrow	
Lannng,	Sarah Emma Preston	
LaRue,	Drucilla Hawkins	
Laster,	Jamina Maples	
Latham,	Margaret	
Lauderdale,	Emma	
Lawson,	Bertha Estell Winchell	
	Sally	
Lawton, OK,	Congregational Church	
	Roseland Extention Homemakers	
Lay,	Edith McAlphine	
Ledbetter,	Vershi Collins	
Ledford,	Sally Christopher Haris	
Ledgerwood,	Grace	
Lee,	Daisy Sims	
	Effie Key	
	Martha Ruth Bell	
	Minnie Agnes Lee	
	Sarah Elizabeth Hicks	
Leecraft,	Mamie	
Leeright,	Mrs. Charley	
Leffler,	Amy Searle	
	Lottie Jacobs	
LeFlore,	* Dreda	
Lehman,	Estelle Winn	
Leib,	Charlotta Survilla	
Lemasters,	Clara Overly	
	Corine Touchtone	
Lemasttus,	Rena Adams	
Lemastus,	Leah	
	Lulu	
Lemming,	Lavinda	
Lemons,	Ora Cambron	
Leonard,	Nellie Francis	
Leseney,	Jane Garbry	
Leslie,	Ruth Rosalee Rigg	
Lester,	Alice	
	Elizabeth Blanche Bath	
Levescy,	Orpha Willard	
	Sterling	
Lewis,	Eva Susan Crockett	
	Ida Lechner	
	* Lettisha Reno	
	Lillian Casteel	
	Sarah Doris Weber	
Liles,	Edith Blaine	
Lillard,	Birdie Woodard	
Lillie,	Susan Ann	
Liming,	Emma Morrow	
Linder,	* Mrs.	
Lindle,	Emma	
Lindley,	Rose Norman	
Lindset,	* Mary	
Lindsey,	Mary Jane	
	Mildred	
Linscott,	* Beatrice Vineyard	
	Fannie Zinn	
Liston,	Iona Garrison	
Little,	Bertha Ruth French	
	Cecilia Haynes	

ittle,	Rose Ann Nancy Parlee
itton,	Mandy Greer
	Sallie M.
ittrell,	Malinda Weger
loyd,	Anna West
ock,	Tennessee Evelyn Monday
	Mary O. McArthur
	Maxine Hefley
ockhart,	Mildred Wells
oftin,	Bennie Lou Coffey
	Cora Johnson
oftiss,	Annie Kuykendall
	Jewell McKissack
ogan,	Ruth Giffith
ogan County,	Lost Creek Church
ollar,	Gracy
omenick,	Luannie Kelly
onestar, OK,	Sunday School
oney,	Dollie Ann Neely
	Adeline
ong,	*Cora Kate Matilda
	Cora Mae
	Mary Elizabeth Dise
	Myrtle Wright
	Sarah
	Virginia
onkford,	Anne Caraline Greensy
oomis,	Stella
orince,	Alice Galloway
outhan,	Gladys
ovdenslager,	Helen Letitia Flaugher
ove,	Lella Callaway
ovell,	Audrey McMining
owe,	Rebecca Tompkins
	Alice Crowe
owery,	Burnice Leib
	Mrs. George
	Zella Victorine Ray
owrimare,	Bessie Davis
owry,	Julia
ucas,	Laura Boyd
	Lula Hale Adams
uke,	Bertha Newby
uker,	T. T.
umberg,	Ann
umpkin,	Erma Godwin
unt,	Jennie Chase
upton,	Dorma Rhodes
	Jennie
weis,	Susie
ynch,	Mattie
aberry,	Malinda Davis
addox,	Ida Morgan
agers,	Mrs. John
ahaffey	Elizabeth Ann Moody
ahaney,	Helen Bell
ahnken,	Lillie
allory,	Fanny
alone,	Sallie Frances Rich
alsbury,	Harriet Smith
alugen,	Alma Johnson
aner,	Cordina
anger,	Juanita Keller
angold,	Flossie Keller
angum, OK,	Farm Women's Club
ann,	Alma Wooten
annsville, OK,	Quilters
antooth,	Nannie Mintor
aple,	*Pearl Judy
aples,	Grace Pursley
arey,	Maude
arland, OK,	Booster Club
arley,	Sarah G. Cooks
arlow,	Jewel Kemmerer
	Josie Fanchier
arlow, OK,	Eastern Star
arple,	*Bessie Shields
	Mable Watkins
	Mattie L. Kyser
	Myrtle
arsh,	
arshall,	Mrs. E. C.
	Louetta Hail
artens,	Bessie Hein
	Maria Bergthold
	Maria Karber
artin,	Trummie Arnold
	Delia F.
	Frances E. Westbrook
	Lenora
	Margaret Gallaher
	Mary Alice Duncan
	Nancy Cantwell
	Onita Finch
	Roberta Hamil
	Sara Jane
	Sarah Wiens
arx,	Mary Gordon
aser,	Sarah Lue Walker
ashburn,	Anna
ason,	Ada A. Butt
assey,	Virgie A. Swing
	Octavia Turner
atlock,	Jewel Adams
Matthew,	Mrs.
Matthews,	Addie
Mattix,	Nora
Maurer,	Louvina Hartle Bausman
Maxwell,	*Effie Maphet
Mayberry,	Dave
	Nancy Jane Frank
	Nanny
Mayer,	Laura
	Lydia Viola Beasley
Mayes,	Della Batch
Mayfield,	Margaret Ethel Cox
Mayhall,	Osy
Mayhew,	Rebecca Burris
Mayhill,	Sarah
Maynard,	Mrs.
Mays,	Edna
	Leona
	Margaret A. E.
Mayton,	Mrs.
Mazey,	Aurora Terwilliger
McAlester, OK,	First Assembly of God Church
	Grand Ave. Methodist Church
	Methodist Church
	Presbyterian Church
McAnally,	Virgie
McBrayer,	Maggie Rogers
McBroom,	Hettie Slagle
McCabe,	Mary Smith
McCaleb,	Lou Ella Hrelchel
McCall,	Blanche
	Morton "Mortie" Price
	Rebecca Edmondson
McCallister,	Dee
McClellan,	Sarah Jane Truesdale
McClalland,	Eliza Jane Fitzhugh
McClendon,	Rubie
McClung,	Florence A. Stouder
McClure,	Eliza Hale
	*Margaret
	Nancy Anne Cranford
McCollum,	*Ethel Alma Watson
McCommas,	Bernice
McCormack,	Katherine
McCormick,	Margaret Weston
McCracken,	Jennie Etta Stewart
McCraw,	Saphronia
McCreary,	Lucy Russell
	Mrs.
McCuddy,	Nellie Blackenstas English
McCuiston,	Sarah Griffith
McCullough,	Stella
McCullum,	Birdie Butcher
	*Ethel Alma Watson
McCurdy,	Emmogene
McCurry,	Ida Louise Reppenhagen
McCurtain, OK,	Home Demonstration Club
McCutchan,	*Pearl Elma Davis
McDaniel,	Ethel Pearl French
	Millia Lemastus
McDonald,	Frances Ellen Wall Dejarnett
	Lennie Ford
	Sara Jane
McDougal,	Dalene Ward
McDougall,	Minnie Wolfe
McDowell,	Lucinda Elizabeth Rogers
McElreath,	Ophelia Collier
	Ruth Gumm
McElroy,	Betty Jane Willoughby
McGaha,	Matilda I.
McGhee,	Evaline Church
	Ida Mae Foster
McGinty,	Peggy Criss
McGowar,	Mrs. John
McGranahan,	*Sarah Foster
McGuinty,	Mollie Pickering
McHair,	Dorthy P.
McInnis,	Esther Alice Hurley
McIntire,	Amanda Caroline Mat
McIntosh,	Clara Belle Neill
	Ethel
	Ollie Worley
McKeever,	Phoebe
McKenzie,	Gladys
	Jennie B.
	Lillian Harower
	Mary
McKinney,	Ada Brock
	Norene
McLaughlin,	Clara Etta Opinghouse
McLauren,	Mamie
McLean,	Maude
	Marvel Pitts
McLish,	*Millie Pickens Pratt
McMichael,	Mrs. Craig
McMillan,	Nora Mitchell
McMining,	Mary Elizabeth Fissler
McNeil,	Philena
McQuillan,	Emma Witter
Medford,	Ruth
Meek,	Mary Elizabeth Perkins
	Numa
	Sarah F.
Meeks,	Allie McKinnon
	Mrs.
Meggs,	Marjorie Patchin
Meler,	Rebecca Evelyne Lee
Mellen,	Salina Belle
Meltette,	Epsy Saunders
Melton,	Lillian
Menasco,	Martha
	Miniola
Menifee,	*Bille Newton
Mensh,	Cordelia Holland
	Geneva
Mentzer,	Mary K. Rhodes
Meshew,	Mrs. Luke T.
Miami, OK,	Indian Quilters
Milburn,	Viola Moore
Miles,	Beulah Glasgow
Millard,	Minnie
Miller,	Emma Malinda Draug
	Fannie Crump
	Fanny
	Florence
	George (Mrs.)
	Hazel Ruth Gary
	Hertha
	Ida Susan
	Inez
	Jennie Mae Glasgow
	J. B. (Mrs.)
	Mamie
	Mary Critchfield
	Mary Louise Nickles
	Minnie
	Opal
	Rosetta Johanna Balster
	*Sarah Elizabeth Schultz
	Sarah Hanna Marshal
	Virgie Lee Dean
	Yetta
Milligan,	Mrs. Lambdin
Mills,	Dora Apple
	Laurinda McGuire
	Martha Montgomery
Millsap,	Ella Alberta Lee
Milspaugh,	*Cora Curry
Minery,	Effie
Misenheimer,	Florence Payne
Mitchell,	Annie Gibson
	Bessie
	Harriet Tescier
	Ida Fay Raaf
	Marie Franklin
	*Minnie Roberts
	Myrtle Irene Bailey
	Sarah Jane
	Viola Brannon
Mizar,	Lydia Mahala Bryan
Money,	Mary Zella Baxter
Montgomery,	Bess
	Jessie Abney
	Leona Stribling Auten
	Lily
	Mrs.
	Mrs. R. R.
	Ruth
	Veola
	Willard
Moody,	Minervia Denham
Moon,	Grace I.
Moore,	Anna Bertha
	Arman Zinda Heyman
	Bertha
	Bertha Johnson
	Bessie
	Elizabeth Falwell
	Elsa Tate
	Eula
	Hugh
	Jennie
	Maggie Stout
	Mary Elizabeth
	Mrs.
	Nancy Pearl
	Trena Marlow
	Wille Mae Wigley
Mooreland, OK,	Methodist Church
Moorman,	Lizzie
	Audrie Lamb
Morgan,	Eliza Jane Jump
	Ollie Arnold
Morlan,	Susan Vice Gassett
Morlay,	Isabelle Wetzel
Morris,	Almeda
	Cuba Peck
	Dixie
	Hazel Walters
	Ida Johnson
Morrison,	Lula Etta Curtis
Morrison, OK,	Community Club
Morton,	Luietta Joy Thomas
	*Susan Ewing
Mosley,	Mary
	Mary Brown
Mosely,	Nancy Jane Williams
Moss,	Esther
Motse,	Lola Hadadys
Mowery,	Dezdy Myrtle Wilson
Moye,	O.
Mozingo,	Mary Harris
Mull,	Mary Elizabeth Knupp
Mullins,	Eva Clara Atkinson
Mulvaney,	Charlotte Evelyn Winn
Munsey,	Mrs.
Munson,	Helen
Murcheson,	Margaret Torrance
Muret,	Maggie Huff
Murphey,	Margaret Arbuckle
Murphy,	*America
	Ida
	Mrs.
Murray,	Bonnie McClellan
	Lillie
	*Lola Oxendine Johnstone
Murrell,	Sophia Barnes
Musgrove,	Myzella Jane Medcalf
Musick,	Cora Helen Norris
Muskogee, OK,	1st Presbyterian Church
Myatt,	Mammy
	Myrtle Edison
	Pamela Vinston
Myrray,	Lillie Marsh
Nagle,	Lenora Armbruster
Nale,	*Helen
	Pearl
Nance,	Amanda Wilburn
	Margaret Hart
Nardin, OK,	Asbury Church Ladies Aid Society
Nash,	Gertrude M. Wolff
Nash, AR,	Methodist Ladies Aid Society
Nash, OK,	Christian Church
Nasworthy,	Effie
Nation,	Mary Loucretia
Naylor,	*Esther Marie Blalock
Neal,	JoAnn Elizabeth
	Rose Ann
Neely,	Maude Mae Lance
Neidig,	Edith Houston
Neighbors,	Martha
Nelson,	*Susie Minnie Gleason
Nemecek,	Lucy Garee
Nesbitt,	Evelyn Rorex
Nescopeck,	Daniel Goodman
Netherton,	Ruth F.
	Bessie
Neugir,	Grannie
Neverburg,	Margaret Ann Tobin
Nevins,	*Ella Sherman
New,	Lena
Newby,	Mary Cathrinne Epperson
	Francis
Newcomb,	Mary
Newhouse,	Mabel Rush Teeters
Newman,	Della Bea Forbes
	Lillie A. Swanson
Newton,	Caroll
	Minnie Ingram
Nicholas,	Rubie Kay
Nicholls,	Callie Brown Lee
Nichols,	*Alice Cockran
	Myrtle Bouman
	Survilla Ann
Nicks,	Clara Ethel Fike
Nicodemus,	Iva Weeks
Niehus,	Alice Gerkin
Niemann,	Linnie Caton
Nightingale,	Katharine Eck
Nikkel,	Agnes Hunricks
Niles,	Jennie Fenimore
Nische,	Lee
Nix,	Annie P. White
Nixon,	Alice Stuart
Noah,	Mattie Lou Carrol
Nobel, OK,	Methodist Church
Noble,	Nettie Lawrance
Noe,	*Leona Kersey
Noel,	Mary Elena Schamp
Nolan,	Rosa
Nolen,	Lola Muir
Nonnamaker,	*Zagonyi Litzenberger
Norman,	Ida Puckett
Norton,	Bertie Harvell
Noud,	Elizabeth Philbert
Nowka,	M.Elizabeth Miller
O' Bryan,	Hettie
O'Clark,	Tassie Overby
O'Donley,	Viola Eagles
O'Kelley,	Mrs. J. W.
O'Neal,	Earie
O'Riley,	Maggie Moore
Ochelata, OK,	United Methodist Church
Odell,	Iva
Odom,	Abba Etta Richardson
Ofutt,	*Mary Piner
Ogan,	Nellie
Oklahoma City, OK,	First Methodist Church
	Kelham Avenue Baptist Church

Oklahoma City, OK	Lutheran Church
Olinburger,	Edith
Olsen,	Alta Maio Baughman
	Carrie
	Dona McCuen
Olson,	Blanche Wheeless
Olvey,	Eva Benson
Orcult,	Rebecca Alice Pearson
Orr,	Harvie Bell
	Rose Cook
Orrell,	Famie Jane Percelly
Osborne,	Jessie McCarter
Ott,	* Mary Jo Ewing
Otterson,	Sarah
Otterstetter,	Friedrika
Outhier,	Nettie Smith
Overholt,	Catherine Firebaugh Heaston
Overton,	Helen
Owen,	Sarah Ellen Michael
Owens,	Sarah Jane
	Marie
Oxendine,	Amanda Howard
Ozmun,	Elizabeth Mary Smith
Padgett,	Deborah
Page,	LaHoma G. George Davis
Palmberg,	Zola Moe Rutledge
Panama, OK,	Fairview Home Demonstration
Parke,	Laura Ann
Parker,	Annice Carlile
	Daisey Ellen Davis
	Lena Bowman
	Mollie Susan
	Ollie Bootner
	Phoebe
Parks,	Ella Catherine London
Parnell,	Iona Acee
Parr,	Verna Cross
Parsons,	* Carrie Hewitt
	Emma
Patchin,	Mary Iona Brown
Patterson,	Cora Hall
	Salena J.
	Susan Melissa Jones
	Susannah Heddrick
	Suzie Moler
	Vertie Mae
	Zora
Patton,	Allie LaRue
	Altus L. Higgins
	Mattie Howard
	Molly Rapp
Pauley,	Molley Martin
Pawhuska, OK,	1st Church of God, Ladies Mission So.
Pawnee, OK,	* Geometry Glass 1935
Paxton,	Frances E. Chapman Griggs
	* Minnie Grace Lehman
Payne,	Mary Ida
	Katherine B.
	Sue
Peachey,	Edna Ray
Pearce,	Fannie Stone
Pearson,	Maggie Stephens
Pedigo,	Charlotte Ann Potter
	Maggie
	Mary Morgan Holman
	Minnie Nancy
Peevey,	Lousia May Upchurch
Pence,	Mary Jane
Pendergrass,	Mary Glass
Penman,	Katie Manns
Pennebaker,	Alice T. Hunt
Pennington,	Penelope Jane Kuhn
Penniston,	Rebeca Jane Frazer
Penny,	Lora
Penson,	Mrs.
Peoples,	Fidelia Kincaid
Perdue,	Mollie Randle
Perkins, OK,	Senior Citizens
Perkinson,	Mrs. Flay
Perrill,	Mary Belle
	Mary Elizabeth Flower
Perrine,	Sarah Davidson
Perry,	Alma Florence Williams
	* Gladys Key
	Ona
Perry, OK,	Presbyterian Church
Peterman,	Charlene Bass
Peters,	Lucy N.
	Martha Elizabeth Tinney
	Frances
Peterson,	Lilla McGowen
	Minnie Dunlap
Petite,	Mrs.
Petr,	Vencencie Novatna
Petty,	Maria
	Willie
Pettyjohn,	* Martha Susan Wolley
	Mrs. M. S.
Pharr,	Lucy
Phelan,	* Camille Nixdorf
Phellips,	Martha Frances Robinson
Phelps,	Elizabeth
	May
Phillippi,	Cora Johnson
Phillips,	* Jane
	Lola
	Mattie May Sires
Pickard,	Maude Davis
Pickens,	Carrie Eudora Sharp
	Nancy Belle
Pickins,	Martha Faries
Pierce,	Effie
	* Iva
	Iva Amanda
	* Lucy
	Minnie Tuttle
Pietr,	V encencia Novotny
Pilgrim,	Mary Virginia Bryan
Pinegar,	Lola Ferne Van Dorn
Pinkston,	Rose Meyer
Pittman,	Family
Pitts,	Mary Belle Young
Platt,	Mary F. Chupp
Ploks,	Amanda Jenkins
Poarch,	Mary Elizabeth Dood
	Susan Dodd
Pocasset, OK,	Arcadia Home Demonstration Club
Poindexter,	Cleta L. Shaw
Polks,	Ruby
Ponca City, OK,	Cross Community Church
Pope,	Emma Busby
Poppins,	Margaret Eye
Pore,	Lula Mae Walker
Porter,	Merie
Porunson,	Mrs. James
Potter,	Alta L.
	Lorine McFatridge
Potts,	Helen
Pounds,	Ella Crum
Poynor,	* Gladys Johnson
	Maude Hamilton
Prater,	Cleo
Pratt,	* Emma Holt
Prescott,	Mrs. T
Price,	Clara Miller
	Minnie Ketterman
Prickett,	Tilley Lynch
Proctor,	Rebecca Bean
	* Rebecca Price
Proserpi,	Rose
Pruitt,	Gertie B. Stephens
	* Sarah Hicks Marshall
Pryor,	Mary Lou
Puckett,	Myrtle Mae Winters
Pulley,	Frances Elizabeth Murray
Pursley,	Nevada Arbuckle
Putman,	Mary Jane
Puttkamer,	Grace
Pybas,	* Lydia Bailey
Pyle,	Bernice
Pyles,	Dorothy Thomas
Quindt,	Amelia Ehrlich
Raaf,	Mary
Rackley,	Marcia Combs
	Narciss
Radabaugh,	Syble May Boudlear
Radley,	Mary Alice Ryan
Rae,	Marge Smith
Ragland,	Eren Kerney
Ragsdale,	Alice Armitage
Raibourn,	Mary Fanning
Raines,	* Ethel
Ramsey,	Eileen
	Etter
Randle,	* Hana Brenton
Randles,	Lulu Dawkins
Randolph,	Mabel Harris MacQueen
Ransom,	Osie Ober
	* Sarah Ellen Eismann
Rasar,	Clara Harris
Rathburn,	Mary May
Ratliff,	Hazel Wheeler
Rauh,	Emma Hacker
Ravia OK,	Ladies Aid Society
Rawlins,	Stella Alexander
Ray,	Emma Irving
	Maria Carnack
	Mary Stiner
Rea,	Rebecca Stimpson
Reames,	Mary Catherine Camplain
Reasons,	Maude
Reber,	Florence Blackwell
Record,	Lela Mae Robinson
Red Oak, MO,	Methodist Ladies Aid
Reddell,	Martha
Reddick,	Della R. Clovis
Redding,	Colleen Kinchen
Reed,	Gertie
	Gertie Jones
	Ida Mozingo
	Laura Burtch
	Lillian
	Lou
	Maggie
	Roy L.
	Vinnie May
Reeves,	Cora
	Rachel Norton
	Rebecca Zimmerman
Regan,	Mary Catherine
Reich,	Wille B.
Reidnour,	Mabel Edna Shaklee
Reiff,	Sarah L. May
Reiger,	Mabel
Reimer,	Mrs. N. J. Penner
Renaud,	Mary Amanda Smith Mangold
Renfro, OK,	Quilting Club
Reppenhagen,	Mary Emmerich
Resler,	Rachel
Resneder,	Dorothy
Revard,	Romanza Mae Nichols
Rexford,	Gertrude Foster
Reynolds,	Elna Bass
	Nancy
Rezny,	Josephine
Rhoads,	Molly Georgia McDaniel
Rhoddy,	Kitty
Rhodes,	Ann
	* Martha Whitfield
	Mary
	Mary Tibbs
Rice,	Sarah Elizabeth Sowers
Riceson,	Esther
Richards,	Ora Fissler
	Dorothy Morris
Richardson,	Mary Lazetta Joyner
Richey,	* Cynthia Ann Williams
Rickabaugh,	Alma Belle Cozine Peck
Ricker,	Jane
	Dora Eyler
Rickett,	* Sarah Bennington
Ricketts,	Ruth E. Shipley
Rieger,	Josephine Mary Amrein
Riley,	Juanita Shaw
	Wauneta I. Couchman
Ringling, OK,	Quilters
Ringold,	Elizabeth McGinn
Ripley, OK,	Church of God
Risner,	Gertrude Wilmoth
	Virginia May Whitlow
Roach,	Bridgett
	May Roddin
	Rebecca Jane
Robbins,	Mae
Roberson,	Alice
	Lucy
	Norm
Roberts,	Annie Jones
	* Ellen Arney
	Ethel
	Etta Melissa Keith
	* Imogene Dennis
	J. Margaret
	Jane "Jenny" Elliott
	Martha Earls
	Martha Richardson
	Mary
	Mary Elizabeth
Robertson,	Frances Emmaline Leseney
	Mallie
Robinson,	Bessie Davidson
	Florence Burwell
	Mary
Robnett,	Bernice Hagar
Rock,	* Emma Kluting Clampitt
Roddy,	Mollie Crawford
Rodgers,	Betty
	Eva Berdella
Rogers,	Bessie Freemont Rodgers
	Fannie May Sayers
	May
	Mrs.
	Nancy Jane Starr
	Ollie Gillespie
	Rose Lightner
Roles,	Edith
Rolla, MO,	Lutheran Church
Roller,	Bertha May Clements
Romshe,	Margaret Griesheemer
Roof,	Rosa Skinner
Rorie,	Ida
Rose,	Bearl Butts
	Eliza
Ross,	Ina Jane McDonald
	Eula Rebecca
	* Martha Ann Mashburn
	Mary E. Coffee
	Ruth M. Brown
	Vergie Kemp
Roulet,	Ada Penny
Rout,	Laverne Graham Cockrell
Rowland,	Mrs. W.
	Mrs.
Rowles,	Harriet Taylor
Ruark,	Elizabeth Catherine Rude
Rudd,	Leona Weisbrod
Rudolph,	Campbell Jane Lockhart
	Laura Edna
Ruff,	Thelma Knowles
Rupp,	Daniel Henry
	Lula Mae Flenter
Rush,	* Lena Seymore
Russell,	Mrs.
	Ruby
	Sally Robinson
Rutledge,	Leroy
	Mary Luella Moore
Rutz,	Alma Johanna
Ryan,	Lela Cave
	Mrs.
Ryker,	Bethel Addis Wolf
Sadler,	Bessie Ellis
Salisbury,	Mrs. W. T. Bearden
Sallisaw, OK,	Methodist Women
Sample,	Ella Weddle Caeley
Sand Springs, OK,	Charles Page Home
Sanders,	Dallas Henderson
	Mattie Catherine Jamison
	Mrs.
Sandifer,	Belle
Sanford,	Florence Clemintine Brodenhamer
	Helen Cooper Lewis
	Lulu
	Mary Jane "Mollie"
Sarchet,	Eva Gilbert
Sare,	Thelma Baughman
Saunders,	Ella
	* Helen
	Juanita Prater
	Mrs.
Saunier,	Jessie Drucilla Meloya
	Mary Lorene George
Savile,	Plen Brawner
Sayers,	Elizabeth Gase
Scates,	Mae Sells
Schamt,	Aeta Johns
Schieffer,	Anna Mae Neverburg
Schiltz,	Mary Iren Desmond
Schmidt,	Helen Martin
	Laura Kirmse
	* Mrs.
Schneider,	Mary Weisse
Schoenhols,	Anna Stabel
Schoolcraft,	Sara Emaline Watson
Schroder,	* Ella Eernissee
Schuelke,	Mrs.
Scoggin,	Alice Burke
Scott,	Harriot
	Laura Mae
	Laura
	Matilda
Scroggin,	Dora Lucinda Steelman
Scroggins,	Jewell Edna Russell
	Mary Elizabeth "Mollie" Potter
Seaba,	Clara Anne Bergman
	Cleo Neoma Beall
Seahorn,	Mrs.
Sears,	Elsie Diathia Buchanan
Secrist,	Cynthia Faye Sutherland
Seidle,	Mellie
Seifert,	Dorthea Luckert
Selby,	Nannie
Sellers,	Martha Meser Smith
Sells,	Faye Jones
Semple,	Minnie Pitchlynn
Senior,	Lillie Bell Slitt
Servere,	Viola Kirchmeier
Sessions,	Audie C.
Sevier,	Alice
Sewell,	Clara Winona
Seymore,	Mary Ruth Atkins
Shaeffer,	Mary Mildred Kays
Shafer,	Mary Parilee Emerson
Shaffer,	* Tabitha Ann Taylor
	Velma Bensch
Shaklee,	Edith
	Harriett Joanna Stalker
Shaller,	Eliza Campbell
Shaner,	Martha
Shank,	Minilee
	* Susan Gall
Shanks,	Olivia Burrows
Shannon,	Mary Katherine Butterfield Davis
Sharp,	Cornelia Drucilla
Sharpe,	Sara Jane Corzine
Sharpton,	Lottie
Sharrock,	Estell Krieger
	Mrs.
Shattuck,	Minnie
Shaw,	Mrs.
	Phoebe Jane
	* Sarah Alice Workman
Shay,	Viola
Sheerer,	Sarah Jane Purvis
Sheese,	Susan Eilen O'Dell
Sheets,	Bertha E. Castello
	Fronia
Sheldon,	Clara
Shellenberger,	* Nancy Ellen Ward
Shelp,	Cleo Ray
Shelton,	Crystal Lowe
	Mariba Walker